Thoughtful Adaptations to Change

Authentic Christian Faith in Postmodern Times

EDWIN F. DREWLO

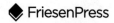 FriesenPress

Suite 300 - 990 Fort St
Victoria, BC, V8V 3K2
Canada

www.friesenpress.com

ISBN

978-1-5255-0458-7 (Hardcover)
978-1-5255-0459-4 (Paperback)
978-1-5255-0460-0 (eBook)

1. RELIGION, CHRISTIAN LIFE, SOCIAL ISSUES

Distributed to the trade by The Ingram Book Company

Dedication

To our four wonderful children and their spouses,
their fabulous children (our grand-children),
and all the people of their generation
who explore the grand vistas
of an authentic Christian faith

TABLE OF CONTENTS

Thoughtful Adaptations to Change

Authentic Christian Faith in Postmodern Times

Introduction

Pastoral church ministry is the special calling to lead a church in its care and development so that individuals become authentic followers of Jesus Christ in the context of a spiritual community constituted by faith in him and empowered by the presence of the Holy Spirit. Properly established and led, the church is the most potent force in the world for good because of the nature of the gospel that is so central to its faith and ministry, and as it has been made known to all of humanity in the Holy Scriptures. The church is the main means by which God's purpose to bring salvation to the world and to establish his kingdom on earth will be accomplished. The story of the church is an amazing chronicle of God's victory over sin and suffering in the world. Amidst incredible odds and despite many difficulties and setbacks, the church has risen to become God's primary human agency for the advancement of the gospel with its many delightful corollaries.

But the church, certainly in its actual geographical locations, is never perfect this side of heaven. Even churches that are well-established and genuine in their application of a consistent, orthodox interpretation of the Bible are on a journey of discovery and development in Christ-likeness. None have arrived, and none are static in their development. The church is either progressing towards the goal of full maturity in Christ, or lapsing into various forms of heretical teaching and self-absorption.

It has been my privilege to be on a journey with the church in general, and with certain ones in particular, since childhood. Due to a deep sense of God's personal calling in my life since the time of adolescence, I have been involved in church leadership for most of my adult life. It has been a profound journey of learning and growing through devotion, informal and formal study, amazing friendships and associations, as well as experiences—both exhilarating and sometimes disappointing. As is true of the larger church, I too have both grown and lapsed at various junctures in my life, but overall, pastoral service in the church has been a very fruitful and fulfilling experience. What has carried me through these years of service in the church has been my deep conviction of the truth of God's self-revelation through the Bible, and especially through the coming of Jesus Christ—the person who fully embodied the very life and character of God himself. As I write, I am most confident that the church will ultimately prevail in the accomplishment of God's purpose to bring all things to completion in Christ, just as he promised (Matthew 16:18). Hopefully, this minuscule contribution can be of some assistance towards that eventuality.

In my work as a pastor, in what I've considered to be a vibrant and evangelically orthodox denomination (the Christian and Missionary Alliance), I have seen a significant change in the nature of church and pastoral ministry. In my time of service in various communities in Western Canada, I have worked with colleagues from many other Christian denominations who have often blessed and challenged my thinking and practice. This has also been the case with those who have been participants in the churches with which I have served. Sometimes I have seen tendencies towards theological liberalism on one hand and what I would call a kind of religious fanaticism on the other. Always the challenge for me has been to seek a thoughtful balance between an accurate biblical understanding, and what we might call a "warm-hearted response" to the generally predictable ministry of the Spirit (as defined by the scriptures).

The changes of which I write in this discourse have happened slowly enough to be almost imperceptible. Yet if one diligently studies the contrast between the life of the average evangelical church in Canada fifty years ago and that of it today, the change is really quite obvious as well as profound. For some time, I have been concerned that many average church participants have not easily understood the reason for the cultural shift happening within the church. Through formal study as well as observation and experience, I think I have been able to discern something of the cultural and philosophical reasons for the changes that have taken place. My sincere desire is to help the larger body of evangelical Christians, who participate in the life of the church week by week and month to month, have a deeper understanding of what is happening in the greater culture. In doing so, my prayer is that Christians may be better equipped to relate to this changing culture in their day-to-day lives, in their church experience, and in their efforts to effectively communicate the Good News in these times.

Another reason for this book is that I wish to speak to the sense of fragmentation that is occurring in the church at this time. There is a good sense of unity within some bodies of Christian believers because the biblical foundations of faith are clearly communicated, understood, and embraced. Along with this, there is a great effort "... *to keep the unity of the Spirit through the bond of peace*" (Ephesians 4:3, NIV). But in some instances, it seems an artificial sense of unity exists based on the adoption of false premises of faith that few are willing to speak against.

Still in other instances, certain congregations are pulled apart by various "winds of doctrine," which often continue without definition or explanation. In some cases, whole denominations end up deeply divided because the theological field is clouded and has shifted in matters that may not seem important at first, but ultimately demonstrate that they are. While some leaders are legitimately calling for Christian charity and unity on grounds of biblical principle, many resist such calls, because they feel they are being asked to compromise on important biblical truths, or the authority of scripture itself. One of the purposes of this study is to give some perspective on why this kind of fragmentation in the church exists, as well as some thoughts on what is necessary for a better sense of organic unity.

It's important to note that even though I am deeply concerned about academic integrity, I am not principally writing for that kind of audience. Primarily because of my pastoral work and interest, I am writing from a pastoral perspective and for the "person in the pew" (one of those colloquialisms that now has lost its meaning because of the uncommonness of "pews"). I have an earnest desire to help ordinary Christians (as well as prospective Christ-followers) understand something of the philosophical and sociological shift that has taken place, so that they might be better able to discern what is positive and what is not. I believe Christ-followers can only more effectively fulfill their calling if they relate a good understanding of the text of scripture to the culture in which they live. After all, it really goes without saying that God's intention is for his people to be fully active participants in his mission to bring his redemptive grace, through the gospel, to the whole world. Usually this won't happen by preaching from a soap box or by handing out "gospel tracts" (even though there may be a time and place for these). More likely than not, it will only happen as we more fully understand our culture, immerse ourselves in it without adopting its values, and then intentionally share the Good News in ways that make sense in our times (all the while knowing that conversion is really God's work).

I am also writing for those who have been called or assigned to responsible leadership in the church. Having been a pastor myself for many years, I am deeply sympathetic with those who have diligently and often sacrificially given their lives to the official service of Christ's church—simply for the joy of serving him. I will have much more to say about this matter near the end of the book, but it certainly is the case that these are very challenging days in the Western world to be serving a church as its pastor. I hope this book will encourage pastors by providing a deeper understanding of the nature of this calling in these days. I hope too that it will strengthen them in their ministry as they gain a better knowledge about the cultural shift that has taken place and what this means for the effective leadership of the church.

As a transition pastor for the past eleven years (following about thirty-five years of resident pastoral ministry in four different churches), serving approximately a dozen different churches for periods of several months to almost a couple of years, much of my work has been with the church's lay leaders. Through it all, I have grown in my appreciation for the significant commitment these people make to the work of the church. As I've worked with them, I've seen them grow in new understanding about what is involved in their roles relative to the pastor's. With more insight and ownership, I've seen them become enthused about this kind of lay leadership despite the cost in terms of time and effort. I try to spend a good deal of time with these leaders helping them find more meaning in their roles by gaining a better understanding of what church leadership means and what effective ministry looks like in the context of today's changing culture.

I realize there is much more to be said, illustrated, and developed on any particular topic in this book. It is far from exhaustive in any sense of that word. My purpose is to provide a general outline of the changes in culture and the philosophical drivers of those changes as best as I have come to understand them. In the process, I hope to stimulate deeper thought and discussion about the changes that have occurred. I am fundamentally a church pastor who is genuinely interested in finding new and better ways to accurately and authentically communicate the relevance of the Christian message not only to those who already are followers of Jesus, so that they can be more fulfilled in living their Christian lives, but also to those who are not so informed, so that they can discover the wonder and beauty of the gospel for themselves.

I need to acknowledge at the outset that what I am seeking to communicate in this book is really the product of input from many different people and sources over the years. Of course, there are my own parents, William and Phyllis Drewlo (now deceased), who led me to faith in Christ and, by their example and instruction, taught me the very basics of what it meant to be a Christian believer. My three brothers and their spouses have also been a substantial factor for good in my life. Over the years, I have been influenced by a large variety of faithful pastors like Joe Wiebe, James McNair, W. H. Brooks, Ernest Bailey, Les Hamm, and William Goetz. I learned a lot about faith and service for Christ from leaders of student ministries such as the Navigators, Inter-Varsity Christian Fellowship, and Power to Change (formerly Campus Crusade for Christ) – especially in my university studies, first at the University of British Columbia and later at the University of Saskatchewan in Regina. But, while still in my twenties, it was the influence of various professors in Bible College and Seminary that taught me to think biblically and theologically. In my year at the Canadian Bible College (formerly in Regina, now Ambrose University, Calgary), it was Professors Murray Downey and Ray Kincheloe, whose passion for evangelism and the ministry of the Holy Spirit, respectively, seemed contagious. It was also during that year that I developed an interest in systematic theology through the teaching of Dr. Samuel Stoesz. After graduating from the University of Saskatchewan in Regina with a BA in Sociology, I enrolled in the newly-minted Master of Divinity program at the Canadian Theological Seminary (also now, Ambrose University in Calgary). There it was that Dr. Rex Boda first taught me to think philosophically. I credit Dr. Albert Cramer with insight about church history and the difference, he said, "between a critical mind and a critical spirit." Dr. David Rambo helped me see the cultural relevance of the scriptures and Dr. John Dahms emphasized the importance of the development of a theology based on good biblical exegesis. There were others, both men and women, who made a huge impact on my life during those years, but these were among some of the most outstanding. And as I entered pastoral work, I benefited greatly from various mentors in the form of colleagues in Christian ministry, especially my good friend, Pastor Ray Matheson, but also Dr. Arnold Cook, Dr. T. V. Thomas, Dr. Bob Rose, Pastor Les Hamm, Pastor Walter Boldt, as well as cross-cultural ministry specialists Frank and Marie Peters, and Richard and Hope Reichert. I also thank God for the valuable friendships of pastoral colleagues such as Arden and Pat Adrian, Ron and Sharon Erickson, Dave and Flora McCarthy, and so many others. I also wish to acknowledge the contribution over the years, of my denominational supervisors (District Superintendents) -- Rev. Alf Orthner (who helped me get started), Rev. Robert Gould, Rev. Arnold Downey, Rev.

Gordon Fowler, Rev. Brian Thom, Rev. David Hearn, and Rev. Errol Rempel.

I am grateful too, for a large variety of individuals in the churches where I have served – Hillsdale (now Living Hope, Regina), North Battleford, Westgate (Saskatoon), and Lakewood (Prince George). I have learned a great deal while serving many churches (mostly Alliance) in transition pastoral ministry for the last dozen years, generally in British Columbia – Dawson Creek, Timbers (Prince George), Quesnel, Ft. McMurray (Alberta), Kitimat, Golden, Cranbrook, Erindale (Saskatoon, Saskatchewan), Trail, and most recently a church of the Mennonite Brethren in Vanderhoof. I am especially indebted to leaders within these churches, professional and otherwise, who have been willing to engage in long discussions about theology, principles of ministry, and practical applications to the church. In similar ways, a number of associates in transitional ministry, chiefly Gerry Teichrob, Cam Taylor, and Daren Wride, also have helped me a lot in these developments.

Near the end of the 1990's, by the encouragement of good friends and my wife, I enrolled in the Doctor of Ministry degree program at Trinity Western University (Langley, BC). In 2005, I was able to complete the modular courses and dissertation of that program at Trinity International University (Chicago). This proved to be a very enriching experience in every good way. I was privileged to be taught by such notables as Dr. Bruce Ware (theology), Dr. Bruce Waltke (biblical exegesis), Dr. Don Carson (New Testament), Dr. Lawson Younger Jr. (Old Testament), Drs. Phil Zylla and Richard Averbeck (spiritual formation), Dr. Paul Feinberg (eschatology), Dr. Guy Saffold (Leadership), Dr. David Larsen (preaching), Dr. Martin Crain (research), and more recently in a graduate audit class, by Dr. David Gustafson (evangelism and missions). I realize, of course, that not everything I have written in this book would necessarily be endorsed by all the people I have mentioned. But this is simply to recognize the large contribution that so many have made to my personal and professional development.

I also want to acknowledge the practical help of the other directors of Second Wind Ministries – Alan Bromley, Charles Claus, Arlo Johnson, and the most recent addition, David Peters. I am very grateful for how these have stood by me through this specialized ministry advancement. It was mainly these who encouraged me to put my thoughts about Christian ministry into writing.

As you will see from the Bibliography, I have also benefited a great deal from other writers, many to which I refer in the book. Partially I write because of what I have known of the profound impact of well-written books in the formation of my own convictions.

Last but not least, I am thankful for my family—our four children and their spouses as well as our ten grandchildren—who by their lives and interests have helped me appreciate much about the times in which we live. My last word of gratitude is reserved for the one with whom I have had the privilege of sharing the grace of life for so many years—my amazing wife, Carolyn. Though serving together in church life and ministry has not always been easy, she has supported me in this role with much grace and candor. It is my hope and prayer that all who read this short study on an appropriate Christian response to the great societal change in our times will benefit substantially and will appreciate the contributions of so many to my own understanding and pastoral ministry development.

Always there is so much more to say about change and postmodernism as addressed in this book. Upon re-reading the draft manuscript many times, I often find there are better ways of saying what I have written. But eventually one has to recognize that what has been written will never be perfect. In the end, I have to commit to its conclusion and leave the final result in God's hands. The writing of the book has been a work of God's grace for me and is presented for his glory. May it be a practical help and blessing to many.

CHAPTER 1

Managing Change

Through the television mini-series *A.D. The Bible Continues, aired on NBC in 2015,* Mark Burnett of reality TV fame (*Survivor, The Apprentice, The Shark Tank*), effectively describes the nature of life for the early Christians in the culture of their time. About that time, for a church worship service sermon, I was asked to focus my attention on the fifth episode of this series, which was based on St. Luke's account of the persecution against the Christians as described in the first few verses of Acts 8. The passage is a classic description of the plight of many Christians throughout the history of the church by which they find themselves in opposition to the prevailing culture and powerbrokers of the time.

Luke's account in Acts describes how the persecution is prompted by the testimony of a little-known church leader of the time named Stephen. He was one of the men chosen in those early days by the church and the apostles to serve the more practical needs of the growing church. These became known as deacons. As a man *"full of faith and of the Holy Spirit"* (Acts 6:5, NIV), it seems Stephen was also blessed with spiritual gifts of miraculous healing and bold preaching. It wasn't long before Stephen found himself having to defend his work before the powerful Jewish Sanhedrin, a large governing body consisting of some seventy-one men.

Like the prophets of a former time, Stephen's "mistake" was to apply the truth of the gospel in a very specific way to the resistant Jewish leaders of his day, saying that they were "stiff-necked," just like their ancestors, in resisting the Holy Spirit. The climax of their sin, he said, was that they were disobedient to the law handed down to them through angels, and that they actually murdered the one whom the former prophets identified as "the Righteous One." Stephen was not particularly politically-correct in making this kind of application, but he didn't seem to be thinking in terms of that societal restriction. His objective was to give the best possible defense of an authentic faith, but his words infuriated the members of the Sanhedrin to such an extent that they took hold of his body, dragged him out of the city, and stoned him to death.

Stephen's death brought a great change to the status of the church and the Christian faith in Jerusalem. Though certainly very costly and sad, Stephen's martyrdom was, in the end, a positive turning point. While the immediate outcome meant untold suffering through persecution for the Christians in Jerusalem, this challenge actually served to accomplish God's intention that the good news concerning Jesus be spread throughout that region. We read in Acts 8:4: "*Those who had been scattered preached the word wherever they went*" (NIV).

This story illustrates many important principles related to life, including the reality and value of suffering, the beauty of boldness in the communication of truth, and the work of the Holy Spirit in ensuring the fulfillment of God's purpose to spread the Good News. But one of the most interesting outcomes of this story is how it illustrates the benefits that a positive adaptation to change can bring to our lives.

Since all of us are familiar with change on many levels, we can relate to this story in a very personal way. In the daily course of our lives, it seems that we are constantly faced with the need to respond to happenings that we didn't anticipate—surprising conversations, news of events in the world that affect our personal lives, sudden losses of one kind or another, accidents, the threat of ill health, and natural disaster. Because we tend to focus on the difficult changes in our lives, we're inclined to overlook the fact that many changes are actually very positive—news of a win, a new opportunity, the birth of a child, or the prospect of a sunny day. Weather, in fact, provides a great illustration of the reality and unpredictability of change. As we say in many parts of the world, "If you don't like the weather, just wait five minutes!" If we take the time to watch the sky for even a few minutes, it is quickly evident that the atmosphere is a world of constant change.

You would think this reality of change in our daily lives would make it easy for us to adapt to change, but the truth is that no matter how much or how often change occurs in our lives, adapting is always a chore. We often look at change as an enemy rather than a friend. We resist change because it makes us feel uncomfortable; it introduces new dynamics into our lives that force us to think and to act. We naturally resist change because it rocks our sense of security. It makes us feel like we're losing control. Often the older we get, the more difficult it is for us to deal with change. Change takes thought, conversation, and energy. Change is painful; it causes stress in our lives. Even good changes can be worrying.

This story illustrates that change, even when it is difficult, can have a very positive effect. We are inevitably stretched through change, but it is that very stretching that can enable us to grow and have a constructive effect on others -- if we adapt positively to it.

While studying change over the past several years in a more personal and intensive way, I was intrigued by the results of a study illustrated by Virginia Satir. Her analysis of change in personal experience is viewed as a series of events that enables a person to ultimately realize significant progress.

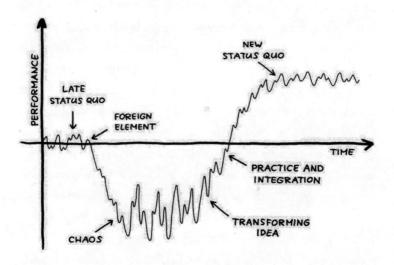

Processing change – Virginia Satir[1]

This illustration demonstrates that personal performance over time can improve because of positive adaptation to change. The main points of the illustration relate to rather definitive personal experiences in which there is initially a downward trend before a more upward movement towards a better experience.

One's experience of the status quo may be fine until some foreign element is introduced into his or her life that has a deeply disorienting effect. Such disorientation will be of varied intensity depending on what it is, a person's personality, one's place in life,

---

1   Jurgen Appelo, *Virginia Satir Change Curve*, licensed by Creative Commons, https://www.flickr.com/photos/jurgenappelo/5201852636, Google Image, accessed on January 2, 2017.

or the nature of the person's spiritual understanding and faith. But the important thing is that it is very real and very disorienting. When this happens, the experience plunges a person for a time (sometimes a long time) into a great valley of chaos. The valley of chaos will undoubtedly consist of many different kinds of emotions, most of them identifiable as various stages of grief—resistance, denial, bargaining, and depression.

Let's suppose a person suddenly loses a relationship through jilted love, a serious disagreement, or sudden death. Those of us who have experienced any of these know all too well how disorienting such an experience can be. As the reality sets in that my job, my spouse, or a friendship is gone, I find myself imagining all kinds of hardships or negative thoughts about my life, the future, or the people who caused it. I may tend to dwell for many days on self-doubt and guilt, or to wallow in the valley of self-pity. I may withdraw from engagement with others, including members of my own family or my church. I find myself asking why, blaming others, and generally feeling disillusioned with life.

But then someone with special grace may penetrate my sullen thoughts with words of hope and encouragement. Perhaps it is a family member, a spouse, or a good friend. It might be an idea from a book, perhaps a Bible passage or story, or possibly a sermon. Suddenly, there appears to be what might easily be considered a transformational thought or event that helps me see that my situation is not as bad as I had thought. Sometimes, of course, a depression from loss will, initially at least, require medical intervention—something not to be discounted in this discussion.

William Bridges writes about this kind of experience in his book, *Transitions: Making Sense of Life's Changes.* Though not writing from a Christian perspective, his main thesis is that transitions follow the course of nature in our own lives. Just as fall and winter must precede spring and summer, so too there are seasons of change in our lives in which we need to endure times of dying to appreciate the sweet times of new beginnings.

Such is the effect of a transformational moment. It enables us to turn our attention from what was to what will be. In transformational moments, we begin to visualize new possibilities, to change our attitude about life, and to start looking forward to the good that is starting to emerge. As we persist along this path, something wonderful and unexpected takes place—our lives begin to take on a new identity, which we increasingly embrace with joy and a sense of anticipation.

The net effect of it all, in brief moments of reflection, is that we are able to see that we have grown more mature, found new purpose, become more productive, and begun to experience life on a whole new level. It all begins with recognizing and adapting successfully to the inevitable changes that are sure to occur in our lives. Just as the Christians of Jerusalem scattered and spread the Good News because of their suffering, so it's possible for God to fulfill his greater purposes in our lives through the changes that he allows or brings. As the Christians of that time adapted to the rather painful changes that must have taken place, so we too can experience the joy of fulfilling God's greater purposes by cooperating with the difficult changes that occur in our own lives.

Part of adapting ourselves to change involves a worldview in which we recognize the existence and intentions of a power or person of greatness, goodness, and strength outside of our lives who can affect our lives for good. Though such a concept is rather intuitive, Christians believe that this power and person is the God who has made himself known—generally through the natural world, but more specifically through the ancient scriptures. This is not the place to provide an extensive defence of the Bible's reliability as an authentic revelation of God's person and plan, but suffice it to say that the Bible has shown itself, through history, archeology, longevity, internal consistency and unity, fulfilled prophecies, and world-wide influence for good, to successfully answer the critics views about what they perceive as its human origins. Most importantly, the Bible details the revelation of a God who sovereignly superintends change in the world and in our personal lives for good through our response to the good news of Jesus Christ.

It is my contention that without a comprehensive and well-developed worldview, the world can appear to be a rather chaotic place in which to live simply because change appears to happen without any kind of reason. This kind of disorientation, one of the characteristics of these times, may easily lead to capricious human behaviour, not to mention serious mental depression and other illnesses. There is an obvious sense in which we were made for order. It's impossible to live in a completely unordered world. But the question remains -- what order?

That query is really the subject of this book. Change has always been of interest to the human spirit, but it seems to be of greater interest in recent times. Partly this is because, at the present time, at least in the Western context, societal change is happening at such an alarming rate that it is difficult for people to adequately process. This is also true for Christians who are seeing great changes take place in their world and especially in the church. The purpose of this book is to try to provide an explanation of the changes that are happening and some suggestions as to how we might adapt to them in positive ways.

For those of us who grew up in the last half of the twentieth century, it is readily evident that there has been a huge shift not only in popular culture, but also in major philosophical thought. Or perhaps it is more to the point to say that philosophical thought conceived earlier has fully come to fruition in our time. We could think of these changes on many levels, such as family values, political ideologies, economics, philosophical ideas, spirituality, and so on.

For example, Fredrick Nietzsche of the late nineteenth century was generally known for his rejection of the notion of absolute truth. His conclusion was that the prevailing motivation for all of humanity had to do with power. Philosophically, his ideas eventually gave rise to what we recognize today as postmodernism, which is largely characterized by a sense of distrust and skepticism. In general, it is evident that Western society has become increasingly self-centered in a way that is characterized by selfish materialism, selfish sexuality, selfish family life, selfish recreational experience, etc.

Meanwhile, Christian ideology and practice has also taken a huge hit, most specifically in the Western world. Though there are many notable exceptions, Christianity and the church are under attack and in rather sharp decline. Though the church of the West does not experience the same kind of persecution as described in Acts 8, it is rather obvious (to those who are willing to confront the facts) that the church is losing ground both in size and influence. As a result, the composition of many churches has shifted towards an older demographic. Thankfully, there are many pockets of spiritual vitality and revival, but it is now painfully evident that those of a younger generation do not attend church in the same numbers as the previous generation.

With all of these changes occurring, one might easily conclude that the church of the West today is under a significant degree of subtle persecution. It represents a change in the status quo of the church's life and experience. Many would be inclined to see this shift as a point of despair. They may tend to turn their attention to prophetic passages of scripture that concern the coming of the last days. They've given up. They are discouraged and sullen. They are distracted. They are inclined to turn from the work of the church and spend their time and resources on other things.

It is praiseworthy, however, that there are others who do not share this spirit of pessimism. Rather than viewing our times as those of greater suffering for the church, they see them as God's hand preparing it for a glorious resurgence of spiritual life and power. Rather than decrying the selfish pursuits of postmodernism and skepticism, they tend to see the potential and opportunity for the current generation to spread the Word of the Lord in greater ways than ever before, just as was true for the early church in Acts 8. In many instances, Christians of the current generation, oblivious to these changes from their perspective, are extremely optimistic concerning the prospects of Christian faith and service.

This book seeks to outline how and why this time of great change could be a season and generation of hope for the church in Canada and the Western world. It is an attempt to realistically describe the breadth of this change and the philosophical reasons for it. But it also is intended to encourage its readers about the opportunities in these times for a powerful witness to the gospel of Jesus Christ. Properly understood and addressed, there is reason to believe that these postmodern times could be an opportunity for great spiritual revival and fruitfulness.

CHAPTER 2
The New World of Postmodernism

Emily is a fictional young woman who grew up in a small city in Western Canada. She is single and around twenty-five years old. From her earliest days, she participated in the life of the church because her parents were strong evangelical[2] Christians. Through Sunday School and Sunday church services, she heard much about Adam and Eve, Abraham, Moses, David, Jonah, and the other prophets of the Old Testament. She also learned much about the

---

2   Since most of my experience has been in the context of the evangelical church, I am writing from that perspective. Evangelicalism was and is a movement, especially of the later 20th century, that has tried to extend the essential nature of the Protestant Reformation stressing the authority of the Holy Scriptures in all matters of faith and eternal personal salvation by an experience of spiritual rebirth -- all based on the Good News of Jesus' death and resurrection for sin. Evangelicalism emphasizes a vibrant experience of Christian devotion that also includes a strong sense of mission. It seeks for the conversion and discipleship of individuals toward the establishment of the church and the expansion of God's kingdom.

amazing person and ministry of Jesus. It is not an understatement to say that she was deeply moved and enthralled by these stories. In fact, while still very young, she recognized the truth of her sin in God's sight and her need to trust in Jesus for forgiveness so she could be at peace with God and have the hope of eternal life. As a little girl, she asked Jesus to forgive her sins and come and live in her heart.

When she entered the eighth grade, Emily qualified to become a participant in the youth group. Under good leadership there, she slowly became more independent of her parents' spiritual guidance and looked for that more from her peers and youth leaders. With her church friends, she regularly attended Friday night youth meetings, participated in Christian summer camp, and went on various retreats and mission excursions. She was taught the significance of baptism as an expression of her identity with Jesus. As a girl of fifteen, despite the challenges from life and others, she decided it was time to express her personal faith through being baptized. It was a great day of celebration for her and her family, as well as a few of her friends who were also baptized at that time.

Emily turned out to be a diligent and relatively successful student in her public school. Not only did she do well in her studies, but she also began to excel in various sports, especially in volleyball. Emily had several good friends who were not confessing Christians. Despite this, she had no trouble identifying herself as a Christian, freely sharing about her church life, and even upholding a commitment to conservative convictions, such as refraining from bad language and not participating in bullying, cheating, and experimentation with drugs. Friends and family respected her for her strong commitment to live as a Christian.

But when Emily graduated from high school and went to university in another city, something changed. She began to see that the world was actually quite different from the world she had grown up in. For one thing, she found it difficult to find Christian friends like those in her hometown. She tried a few different churches similar to the one she had known since childhood, but generally speaking, the people seemed preoccupied with their own friends and weren't exactly looking to reach out to people like her. She took initiatives to connect with people of her own age, but they too seemed more intent on their established friendships. After a while, Emily found it difficult to continue going to churches where there didn't seem to be much interest in her. Besides, even though the churches she attended were of a familiar tradition, she found some of their expressions of worship awkward and superficial. Her attendance became more sporadic and eventually she dropped out altogether.

Then there was the university itself and her course of studies. At first, Emily found it difficult to make connections for many of the same reasons it had been difficult to find friendships in the church. In this larger context, she heard rather negative references by professors and students to Christianity and the church. This wasn't totally surprising to her, since she had grown accustomed to a lack of enthusiasm about the church among her peers while still in high school. But in the university context, she found the criticisms stronger and more direct. The Christian faith, some inferred, was actually responsible for many of the problems that existed in the world, such as colonialism and today's environmental problems. Some spoke of Christianity and the church as being prejudiced, somewhat exclusive, and opposed to the discoveries of modern science.

It's fair to say that her new experience and exposure caused serious doubts to arise in Emily's mind. Perhaps her Christian faith was merely the result of having grown up in a Christian family. Would she be a Christian if she had been born in some other part of the world? Could it be that the positive claims of the faith she had come to know were skewed in some way? For example, maybe there was more to the idea of evolution and natural selection than she had previously considered. And if so, what did that say about the reliability and authority of the Bible, which spoke in terms of a seven-day creation?

While all of this was going on in Emily's mind, she observed that the non-Christians she had come to know at the university seemed to have a positive attitude about life's challenges and were trying to make the best of their world through "enjoying the moment." Increasingly, she began hanging out with them. While still holding on to some of her conservative values, she found herself becoming progressively open to non-Christian ways of thinking. Maybe, for example, if you were really in love with someone, it didn't matter so much if you spent the night together for sex. In some circumstances, she began to imagine that abortion wasn't always wrong. And since some animals occasionally appeared to display an inclination towards same-sex attraction, couldn't this also legitimately be the case in some human relationships?

The lack of a good Christian community where her faith could be strengthened, combined with the doubts and questions that arose from her studies and new non-Christian friendships, all served to slowly turn Emily in a new direction. Unfortunately, she didn't have the influences and essential academic and spiritual resources to provide good answers to the doubts or criticisms that began to emerge. Eventually, Emily fell in love with an attractive young man who didn't have any of the Christian beliefs and training with which she had grown up. Though her family was deeply concerned about the changes they saw in Emily's life, they felt powerless to provide any adequate resistance to this new trajectory. Having lost all sense of control over Emily's life, they determined to resolve their deep suffering by continuing to love her as best they could, and to pray for her, trusting that God would be faithful to his promise to eventually prevail in her life.

In many ways, Emily is a caricature of what is happening in the lives of many young people today who have grown up in strong evangelical or other Christian environments. Though there are many notable exceptions, both of churches who rise above these trends and of individual young people who prevail despite the discouragements to faith that come their way, more often than not, the new generation is seduced by a spiritual Enemy who effectively uses current philosophy and popular culture to turn them away from their biblical faith, and in the process, also greatly weaken the church.

This generalization about a fading sense of faith among Gen-Xers and millennials is not mere conjecture. If one thinks of the issue anecdotally, or begins to examine local church and denominational statistics, they will quickly come to realize that active participation in the church in Canada, especially by millennials, is definitely in decline.

A couple of years ago, *The National* of the Canadian Broadcast Corporation, produced an item entitled "Are We Godless?" Journaled by Chris Brown, it reported on trends in the Canadian faith scene.[3] He documents that on one hand, religious faith has increased due to burgeoning immigrant populations, but on the other, it has significantly declined due to the rise of secularism. While there is a continuing interest in spirituality in many forms,

---

3   Chris Brown, "Religion in Canada: Are We Godless?" *National News*, directed by Peter Mansbridge, (Toronto: Canadian Broadcast Corporation, May 13, 2015.), television.

orthodox Christian faith has waned. At the same time, Roman Catholicism has been bolstered in Canada by new immigrants, 20 per cent of whom adhere to the Roman Catholic faith. Also significant, according to Brown, is that evangelicalism has remained relatively static at 11 per cent of the Canadian population. There is evidence of decline among the older ("mainline") Christian denominations in Canada, so it is evident that secularism is definitely on the rise in Western culture.

Other statistics are not as generous regarding evangelicalism in Canada. Pew Research in June 2013 made the following observation and conclusion:

> Two-thirds of Canadians (including adults and children) identify either as Catholic or as Protestant, but both Christian groups have seen substantial erosion in their shares of the Canadian public, according to the analysis by the Pew Research Center's Forum on Religion & Public Life. The percentage of Canadians who identify as Catholic has dropped from 47% to 39% over the last four decades, while the share that identifies as Protestant has fallen even more steeply, from 41% to 27%.[4]

This trend is significant. Though there certainly are individual anecdotal exceptions to this drift, there is no doubt that the increase of "nones" (those unaffiliated with any Christian church) makes a change of this nature noteworthy. The trend is similar in the US. In

---

4   "Canada's Changing Religious Landscape," Pew Research Center, http://www.pewforum.org/2013/06/27/canadas-changing-religious-landscape/. Accessed January 7, 2017.

May 2015 Pew Research had this to say about church attendance in the US:

> ... the major new survey of more than 35,000 Americans by the Pew Research Center finds that the percentage of adults (ages 18 and older) who describe themselves as Christians *has dropped by nearly eight percentage points in just seven years,* from 78.4% in an equally massive Pew Research survey in 2007 to 70.6% in 2014. Over the same period, the percentage of Americans who are religiously unaffiliated —describing themselves as atheist, agnostic or "nothing in particular"— has jumped more than six points, from 16.1% to 22.8%. And the share of Americans who identify with non-Christian faiths also has inched up, rising 1.2 percentage points, from 4.7% in 2007 to 5.9% in 2014. Growth has been especially great among Muslims and Hindus, albeit from a very low base.[5]

Further research confirms this trend. Tim Keller has written about it as well. He refers to a study published by Putnam and Campbell in 2010.

> ... from 1970 to 1985, the number of young adults (eighteen to twenty-nine) who called themselves evangelical rose from 19 percent to 26 percent,

---

5   "America's Changing Religious Landscape." Pew Research Center, http://www.pewforum.org/2015/05/12/americas-changing-religious-landscape/. Accessed May 12, 2015.

while the number of young adults who said they
have "no religious preference" declined somewhat, from 13 percent to 11 percent. However,
over the last twenty years, we have seen this
trend reversed. The percentage of young adults
who marked "no religious preference" rose to
nearly 30 percent, while the percentage of young
adults calling themselves evangelicals plummeted
toward 15 percent. Putnam and Campbell report,
"In the mid-1980s, evangelicals had outnumbered
nones among American twenty-somethings by
more than 2:1, but by 2008... young nones outnumbered young evangelicals by 1.5 to 1.[6]

Something similar has happened in the denomination with which
I am affiliated—the Christian and Missionary Alliance of Canada.
In 2011, the number of people in attendance at Alliance churches in
Canada was 85,855. By 2013, that number remained essentially the
same at 85,848. It did go up to 90,436 in 2014 but then down again
to 88,847 in 2015. And, at 435 for 2015, the number of churches has
also remained relatively static over the five-year period (inclusive)
from 2011 to 2015.[7]

---

6   Robert, D. Putnam and David E. Campbell, *American Grace: How
     Religion Divides and Unites Us* (New York: Simon and Schuster, 2010),
     quoted in Tim Keller, *Center Church: Doing Balanced, Gospel-Centered
     Ministry in Your City,* (Grand Rapids: Zondervan, 2012), 184.

7   Statistics provided by Dave Freeman, vice president, Canadian
     Ministries, the Christian and Missionary Alliance in Canada, January
     25, 2017.

Though there are exceptions, it is evident that the general trend for the church in North America, including those of an evangelical persuasion, is one of decline. While the church did see a small measure of resurgent growth in the latter part of the previous century, this pattern has not been sustained.

Statistically speaking then, the trend has not been favourable towards what we might call a burgeoning Christian faith culture in the Western world. In fact, it is quite the opposite. In the next chapter, we'll consider some more particular examples of the trend away from vibrant faith in Western culture.

CHAPTER 3
Signs of Change

As I begin writing this chapter, I am looking out on a world whose season is rapidly changing right before my eyes. Just a week ago, a walk in the wooded paths near our home offered a glorious display of lush green growth in the bright warm sunshine of the day. Yesterday, however, that same walk made it very obvious that we had turned a seasonal corner. Cooler nights and fewer hours of warm sunshine during the day had slowed the flow of nutrients to the leaves of the trees, causing many of them to turn from bright green to yellow or even red. A subtle but rather rapid change was happening right before my eyes.

Life and history are far from static. Heraclitus, the Greek philosopher, described it graphically when he is reported to have said, "You can never step into the same river twice." Someone else has said, "The only constant in life is change." It is an inescapable reality of the natural world and the human experience that change is taking place all the time. Even the atoms of any molecular (solid, physical) structure, we have come to realize, are in a state of constant motion and change.

The irony in this is that there is an important sense in which the human spirit invites and actually welcomes change. None of us wish to live in a changeless world. We were made for change and adventure. We long to grow and to see our children grow. Furthermore, we take initiatives to see change happen in our physical lives, our personal sense of well-being, our communities, and our nations. We are strongly motivated to be agents of change. We like to set out on new courses of travel, adventure, education, work, and experience. We love the idea that we can have influence on others, perhaps even to the point of setting a new societal direction for good.

On the other hand, there is something in all of us that resists change, especially if it happens too rapidly or takes us in a direction with which we are uncomfortable. Independent, self-willed, and stubborn beings that we are, we only tend to favour relational or social change if those changes agree with our disposition or personal interests. For the most part, we find ourselves constantly having to relate, adjust, and/or adapt to change. Often rather than being agents of change, we feel we are its victims. Depending on the degree and direction of the change involved relative to our own well-being or opinion, such an experience can be either very stressful or exhilarating.

A further factor complicating how we relate to change concerns one's own actual aging process. It's a fact that the older we grow, the more inclined we are to seek stability in our personal life experience. Security in relationships, work, finance, and geographical location become increasingly important as we grow older. That's why a younger generation is more interested in, and adaptable to change. That is also why young people are often at the forefront of change. Personal security is much less of an issue for a person who is young, simply because they have less to lose. They have not yet had the opportunity to establish much of any great value. But older persons, those in their fifties or sixties, feel that there is much more at stake in risking an initiative for change or in sustaining one that seems forced upon them.

There is, then, this sense of tension between the generations (maybe even real conflict) in their perspectives regarding change and how to relate to it. A classic example in the church has to do with styles of worship. The "worship wars," as they have come to be called, emerge when an older generation seeks to retain the use of classical hymns while a younger generation wishes to be innovative in worship through the use of more recent lyrical and musical creations.

Clearly my own interest in this subject and the reason I write is because I am now analyzing all of this from the perspective of someone who has been on life's journey for a while. I freely admit that while I am most interested in the innovations of a younger generation and the direction of today's expression of faith and church life, I have a bias towards expressions of the faith with which I am more familiar and comfortable. Thus, rather than readily embracing the changes I see in today's church, I am inclined to offer a critique of innovative expressions and practices, because many times they do not appear to match the theology and faith I feel is more accurate and genuine. Nevertheless, I also recognize that it is entirely possible for such bias to be prejudiced by personal interest or a skewed perspective. Even as I question the faith innovations of today's generation, I need to be willing to recognize the wisdom of some change as I diligently study the reason for those changes. What I mean is that it is important to engage in a process of critique from the perspective of a humble heart and properly critical mind.

Another peculiar element in this process is that a younger generation doesn't typically think of the processes of change in the same way an older one does. This is simply because young people do not have the advantage of comparison peculiar to an older generation. As a result, they tend to be less analytical about social change and simply, often quite unconsciously and uncritically, fully engage in the changes that are taking place.

An additional factor, unique to today's generation when it comes to analyzing the changes that have taken place, concerns the major subject of this book—the reality and implication of the move from modernism to postmodernism. By its very nature, the modernism that came out of the Renaissance was committed to structuralism. Its pride was in the fact that the human mind had the capacity to rationalize and systematize everything, including philosophy, science, history, and theology. My own generation coming out of the last half of the twentieth century was conditioned to think in these terms. By contrast, the postmodern generation has tended quite blatantly to reject that kind of structuralism and systemization. The modus operandi of today's generation is that the reference points of modernism don't actually exist. More to the point, those "absolute" reference points were a way of ordering the world in order to empower people to subjugate the less powerful. This generation actually interprets modernism as having been sinister and evil, and negatively labels it as colonial and imperialistic. This reality will be developed in a later chapter.

Today's generation has a bias against the kind of analysis that characterized the modern period. Since their philosophical position is that life is rather irrational, today's younger people don't, and really can't, appreciate the idea that a term like postmodernism represents. One is more likely to hear an older generation speak of postmodernism and its effect rather than postmoderns themselves. This is also because of how millennials tend to think about history in general—as a caricature of the dominant culture's perspective. The fact is, especially from the viewpoint of a typical modernist, there has been a radical shift in the way people think and live. It is a cultural shift of large proportions, so much so that an earlier generation is somewhat frustrated in their attempt to understand and appreciate it, even as it comes to participate in it. Some typical expressions of this cultural shift include the following:

Styles of Dress

One of the more obvious and initial signs of philosophical change in popular culture concerns styles of daily dress. These changes are generally quite incremental, but it doesn't take any kind of scientific study to show that in recent years there has been a notable shift in personal attire towards a more casual appearance including, for example, the ubiquity of wearing deliberately torn or worn-out jeans. This casual trend in fashion is true for the general population, but for the purposes of this book, it is also interesting to see how this change is evident in the church.

During the sixties and seventies, and even well into the eighties, it was quite unusual to find people coming to church in casual dress. Pastors, including me, led public worship services dressed in rather formal attire—suits and ties. Women's dress also followed more traditional patterns. Worship itself was led by a person more formally dressed, standing behind the podium or pulpit, often with others standing near to assist with worship (sometimes even a choir of men and women dressed in "choir gowns"). The pastor and other leaders of the service were seated on the platform to the right and left of the pulpit.

During the nineties and into the beginning of the twenty-first century, it became increasingly common for pastors and worship leaders, as well as participants, to be dressed much more casually. This change was somewhat geographically oriented in that it was more apparent towards the coastal regions of the country rather than in the more central regions of the continent. (Historically, apparently, it has not been uncommon for the western frontier to be generally more innovative and liberal than its continental counterparts.) This pattern was slower to develop in more traditional Christian churches, but Christians in the evangelical tradition, with its emphasis on grace, instead of rules and regulations, moved quickly in this direction, keeping pace with the same trend in the popular culture. Today it is not uncommon to find many church leaders in evangelical churches wearing jeans (or shorts) and T-shirts, whether while leading public services or during their regular office hours (if they have "office hours").

The congregants of evangelical churches have also become increasingly casual in dress, conversation, punctuality, and their actual participation in the worship service. Most people today place small value on formal dress for something like church. They would be quick to say that what's on the inside of a person is more important than what is on the outside. Besides, none of us are in any position to judge a person's heart or motivation. The capacity to judge anyone's heart is God's prerogative alone. Actually, postmoderns would remind us, if we understand scripture properly, that God seems more kindly disposed towards those who are of a humble heart and who readily distance themselves from expressions of pretension. Sooner or later, one might well ask what may have precipitated this change.

As mentioned, this casualness in dress also extends to other aspects of worship practice, like punctuality and consistent attendance. Today's congregants, due to ease of mobility and other outside interests, are much more sporadic in their attendance often participating in less than two-thirds of the church's worship services each month. It is readily evident that this factor has a huge impact on volunteer ministry, the strength of community, and church finances, not to mention the pastor's opportunity for an effective preaching or teaching ministry.

Music

The evident shift in personal fashion is but a small indication of a much larger change affecting many other cultural expressions. In general, the careful observer will note that various art forms of personal expression are much more varied and eclectic. There is less conformity to traditional forms of popular culture. This is also evident in the way people express themselves in music, in various forms of artistic entertainment, in personal language and speech (for which there are also ever more opportunities on social media), as well as in such things as hairstyles and body imagining (personal tattoos, hair-colouring, and body-piercings).

I am especially interested in how this shift has affected church worship styles. In many ways, different expressions of worship in the late 1980s and following were at the forefront of the "worship wars" between moderns and postmoderns. That's because music is such a prominent art form in general, and especially so in the context of church worship. Christians have always had deep feelings about what is appropriate in ascribing corporate praise to God. Moderns have been inclined to defend what they have considered to be the musical grandeur and theological depth of the traditional hymns of the church. But in these postmodern times, hymn-books with words corresponding to musical staff lines and notes, have given way to lyrics sequentially posted on a video-animated screen and a musical melody that can only be learned by ear and

ʷᵛ   ıs change, due in part to technological advance, has
        .nenal.

        ѕe one of the most important values of postmodernism
        ʼs authenticity, the preference of today's generation is for
a much more organic feel to its worship expression, resulting in,
for example, the proliferation of songs that are written by local
talent. Also, one finds that today's worship songs are often more
like ballads or testimonials written in free verse. As well, the focus
in worship centers more on an emotional connection with God
rather than a cognitive one in consideration of God's attributes or
redemptive activity.

This change in focus is also demonstrated through a greater
sense of emotional intensity in worship, often demonstrated by
increased repetition or electrically-generated volume. Rather than
depending on one main instrument (the piano or organ), worship is
enhanced using many kinds of instruments, including guitars, wind
and string instruments, as well as percussion. Many more people
aspire to be original musicians without ever becoming formal students of music. To the postmodern mind, one of the most essential
elements in any valid endeavour is passion. In a way, since rationalism is a product of the modern period, it seems evident that the
cognitions of the mind for postmoderns are less important than the
feelings of the heart. Much has already been written about these
changes but it is worth noting in this context.

Spirituality

One of the effects of the rationalism of the modern period was
a strong emphasis on a logical approach to the understanding of
faith. This emphasis bolstered Christianity, because in many ways

there is much about the Christian faith that is based on well-developed reasons for the existence of God, the reliability of the biblical record, the gospel itself, the nature of the Christian life, and the history of the Christian church.

However, with the dawn of postmodernism and its challenge to the rationalism of the modern period, there has been less appeal to reasonable arguments for the existence of God or even the reliability of the Bible. Thus, an approach to faith began to develop that came to be known as pluralism. This approach simply affirmed that Christianity was merely one of many different ways in which people might relate to God. Ultimately, the conclusion of postmodern thinking was that since the idea of truth was rather relative, faith was a matter of individual perspective or preference.

This also shows up in how postmoderns regard the matter of public prayer. It was common, in the modern period for example, at least among confessing Christians, for prayer to be a regular practice during family meal times. But the anti-structuralism of the postmodern perspective often overlooks not only meal-time prayer but the family meal-time itself as vestiges of mere formality. Because of erratic work schedules and the ubiquity of electronic media, in many instances there is a greater sense of casualness about daily structured family times.

Yet, spirituality itself in this postmodern time appears to be of much greater interest than it had been to the general population of the modern period. The subject finds its way more readily into daily conversations during this time, for example, through general references to prayer. In fact, Christians are more readily inclined to pray for one another on the phone, in restaurants, or on the street. No doubt, this is because the rational structuralism of the modern period has given way to more informal and emotional ways of thinking and speaking. Also, with the current emphasis on tolerance, people generally are more open about identifying their own faith perspective as well as allowing for other expressions of faith. And, contributing to this spiritual reality is globalization, which has resulted in more exposure and connection with people of other religious traditions. While skepticism towards Christianity, especially in the Western world, has grown stronger, people are generally more spiritually conscious and engaged. The implications of this change will become clearer in a later chapter.

Morality

Morality is a general word that refers to standards of conduct that people regard in relation to one another in our society. Quite phenomenally, every culture in the world intuitively seeks to establish mores that are directed towards the prevention of such things as disrespect, murder, stealing, lying, and sexual abuse. On the positive side, morality is concerned about respect and care for one's neighbour, especially their family members. The most primitive peoples imaginable have societal customs in place that effectively censor aberrant moral behaviours. Christian theology affirms that these kinds of moral laws are intuitive, because God's laws have been established in the human psyche by God's design (Romans 2:15). As a result, the highly Christian-influenced cultures of the West, in the past, have established detailed laws that are especially designed to prevent various kinds of immorality. Beyond the existence of constituted laws of this kind, there are all kinds of social customs that render certain behaviours as more, or less, acceptable.

This is especially true in relation to moral standards regarding sexuality. During the modern period, people's sexual behaviour conformed to traditional standards. No doubt owing to the strong influence of Christian teaching up to that time, sexual expression was regarded as properly legitimate within the confines of marriage, defined as a lifelong commitment between a man and a woman. Certainly, there were all kinds of aberrations and secret practices to this general standard in Western society, but the structuralism of the time maintained a fairly consistent commitment to the legitimacy of sexual expression within the institution of marriage. Consistent with other cultures throughout the world, marriage itself was regarded honourably as a vital social establishment.

With the emergence of postmodernism in popular culture, however, prevailing attitudes regarding sexual conduct began to shift towards a more ambiguous definition of sexual expression. As late as June 1999, the Canadian House of Commons passed a motion by something like four to one that the traditional definition of marriage should stand:

> That, in the opinion of this House, it is necessary, in light of public debate around recent court decisions, to state that marriage is and should remain the union of one man and one woman to the exclusion of all others, and that Parliament will take all necessary steps within the jurisdiction of the Parliament of Canada to preserve this definition of marriage in Canada.[8]

However, only six years later (July 2005), the government of Canada passed a new law that effectively replaced that earlier

---

8   Canada. Parliament. House of Commons. "Marriage." Edited Hansard Debates. 36th Parl., 1st Session. Number 240. (June 8, 1999),   http://www.ourcommons.ca/DocumentViewer/en/36-1/house/sitting-240/hansard.

one. The new law recognized marriage in a much broader way: "Marriage, for civil purposes, is the lawful union of two persons to the exclusion of all others."[9]

This change in the definition of marriage accurately reflects the change towards sexuality adopted by the broader Canadian society during this period. Of course, the biggest application was the legitimization of same-sex relationships, but attitudes regarding more sexual freedom outside of the traditional definition of marriage began to flourish as well. Not surprisingly, one of the changes in this new postmodern period has been in the matter of sexual expression and freedom. This is evident in the fact that today there is less social stigma associated with conversation about sex, engagement in premarital sex, incidence of abortion, and the promotion of explicit sex education in the public schools among younger and younger students. Regarding the institution of marriage itself, weddings may not exist at all, or may be constituted more simply, perhaps without a formal (church) ceremony, or to what is now simply referred to as a "common-law" union with legal status.

Recently, the national news in Canada reported on the interest some have in legalizing polyamorous "marriages" for the sake of protecting the rights of partners and children in those relationships. Polyamorous relationships are those in which men and women in an existing co-habiting relationship allow one another to have other similar relationships. The identification of this reality and the desire to legitimize such illustrates the huge changes that have occurred in sexual morality and attitudes.

---

9   "Civil Marriage Act," *Justice Laws Website, Government of Canada,* accessed January 2, 2017, https://lop.parl.ca/About/Parliament/ LegislativeSummaries/bills_ls.asp?ls=c38&Parl=38&Ses=1.

Because the church has traditionally stood at the forefront of teaching about sexual morality based on the Bible and historical Christianity, it has been increasingly marginalized and even maligned by a society that has moved much further towards less traditional expressions of human sexuality. Accordingly, there has been more pressure on the church, already in the early stages of these postmodern times, to be less restrictive about the nature of marriage and sexual expression. Liberal elements in the church have been inclined to be more open towards various expressions of sexual freedom, including heterosexual unions without formal covenantal marriage, premarital sex, and even same-sex unions. On the other hand, churches that place a strong emphasis on the authority of the Holy Scriptures have continued to work hard at maintaining a commitment to what is understood as God's design for sex within the confines of covenantal marriage between a man and a woman.

Even the most casual observer of societal trends in the last fifty years will quickly conclude that there are many other signs of radical change regarding how people think and live in the culture of our times. There are many other changes in western culture in the last fifty years that have not been mentioned – cooking, diet, family life, work, child-rearing, education, health care, senior care, vacation, personal finance management, and a host of others. It's easy to conclude that many of these changes are simply due to the large technical and economic shifts that have characterized this period. Granted that such features are significant factors in the speed of these changes, I believe it is evident that a deeper and far more significant factor drives the shift that has taken place at a philosophical level. It is this shift to which I now wish to turn the reader's attention.

CHAPTER 4

The Development of Postmodern Thought and Culture

It is obvious to almost everyone, especially when it is drawn to their attention, that there have been huge changes in popular culture in the last fifty years, but few people are aware of or even think much about the reasons for this shift. Some would consider the changes to be progressive and the natural outcome of greater educational or technological advance. Others would see a relationship between these changes and the advancement of various scientific theories, such as the evolution of the human species or the possibility of life on other planets. Still others, especially from a more Christian perspective, would simply call it, "a sign of the times." Further along this line is the idea that "the ruler of the darkness of this world," as Saint Paul speaks of him in Ephesians 2, is controlling the machinations of human hearts and minds to push these changes.

While there undoubtedly is a great deal of truth in all of these explanations the purpose of this study is to look at these changes from a sociological and philosophical perspective. This may be due to my own continuing interest in sociological trends. Combining this curiosity with one that also traces the development of philosophical ideas not only provides a reasonable explanation for the reasons for current trends, but ultimately leads to a better understanding of how to relate the Christian message to the culture and people of our times with a view to more successful Christian ministry. In other words, this study is not merely about information on a theory of sociological trends, but it is also about providing some practical ideas on how to more effectively communicate the wonderful good news about God's redemptive plan in Christ for all of humanity. More will be written about this towards the conclusion of the book.

Some years ago, Michael Frost and Alan Hirsch addressed the changes that have taken place in our society in their book, *The Shaping of Things to Come*. They wrote about what they described as the demise of Christendom in the Western world. They postulated that while Christianity existed as an institution since the time of Constantine in the fourth century, by the close of the twentieth century, it was evident that it no longer occupied the center of Western thought and practice. Their thinking aligns with this idea that a major shift has taken place in our society. As an evangelical church pastor seeking to lead a series of churches at the close of the last century and the beginning of this one, I have personally witnessed the reality of the shift that Frost and Hirsch speak about. Church happenings, including pastoral transitions, used to be prominent in community newspapers. News of the arrival or departure of a new pastor in the community is no longer news. In today's world of commerce Sunday is like any other day of the week. The church bell no longer tolls at the center of the town square. Bible reading and the Lord's Prayer are certainly no longer a part of the daily routine in the public-school classroom. In many other ways, it is certainly evident that the church no longer occupies the center stage of life in North America. The question is, why?

Pre-modernism

It's possible, I believe, to distinguish three great movements in the development of philosophical thought in Europe and the Western world. The first movement may be referred to as the pre-modern period. In pre-modernism, the dominant philosophical perspective was greatly influenced by Greek, Jewish, and Christian thought. The Greek influence came by way of Plato and Aristotle, who conceived the idea of a kind of order in the universe that might be understood in terms of certain rules of logic. Jewish and Christian thought built upon this idea of revelation through nature in a more particular kind of God's self-disclosure. Though various church fathers such as Origen and Ignatius developed these ideas in the early part of the Christian period, it was Thomas Aquinas of the thirteenth century who could be said, through his writings and systematization, to best represent the dominant philosophy of this pre-modern period, which lasted until about 1650 A.D. It was Aquinas who spoke of God as the *prime mover*, or first cause of all things.

The primary philosophical tenet of the pre-modern period is the idea of a transcendent (totally independent) being who is knowable through some form of revelation. The Christian church, in that time, largely existed as an extension of the Roman Empire. It emphasized God's self-revelation through nature, the Holy Scriptures, and its own authority. The idea of God's existence and his self-revelation were central to the development of Western culture during this period. It was a time in which church authority was formative and dominant, thus contributing to the development of the idea of Christendom. All of this was reflected in the construction of great cathedrals and churches throughout Europe during this time. It also involved a way of life characterized by more agrarian forms of existence, thus making people feel a greater sense of dependence upon divine assistance.

I'm sure it is fair to say that this period was also characterized by what we might refer to as religious quackery or superstition. It was a time of general illiteracy, most everyone being wholly dependent upon church leadership for spiritual understanding and direction. The common people of the day developed their own ideas of spirituality, blessing, and cursing. Some of these ideas, combined with a good deal of corrupt Christian theology of the time, resulted in various forms of religious syncretism. Nevertheless, the church and its authority tended to be quite central to life and culture during this period. One could say that the pre-modern time was characterized by the importance of the consciousness of God, though often not in an accurate or attractive manner.

Modernism

Around the mid-seventeenth century, influences and questions emerged that began to turn the tide of philosophical thought. The beginning of these changes in mediaeval thought came through philosophers such as Erasmus, Thomas More, and Francis Bacon. Erasmus, who lived from 1466 to 1536, challenged many of the traditions of the church and popular superstitions of his time. As a rationalist, he was willing to question notions of spirituality promoted by the church in that era. Thomas More (1478–1535), a friend of Erasmus, is often credited for being the father of modern socialism, because he proposed an imaginary land of ideal social conditions called *Utopia*. In so doing, he challenged hierarchical ideas promoted by the church of the medieval period. Francis Bacon (1561–1626), on the other hand, was an Englishman who emphasized the importance of inductive reasoning to come to conclusions about the world. He is often credited with being the father of modern scientific research because of his introduction of the scientific method.

One can readily see how these influences paved the way for a more inquisitive approach to life that came to characterize what we now describe as the modern period. It began about the time of the early seventeenth century and came to more complete fruition in the writings of the French thinker, René Descartes (1596–1650). His skepticism of various theories of knowledge led him to the conclusion that humankind's understanding was rooted in its own consciousness. His famous dictum, "I think; therefore, I am," became a way of summing up the dominant philosophy of the modern period.

A significant development in the early part of this period concerned the various theories of reality that challenged the conventional thinking of the church. The classic example of this was Copernican thinking about the nature of the universe. Though deeply involved as a cleric in the church of his time, Nicolas Copernicus (1474–1543) theorized that the earth rotated on its own axis once daily and travelled around the sun once yearly. This was a revolutionary idea in more ways than one, because up to that time everyone believed, based on the church's teaching, that the earth was the center of the universe and that everything else revolved around it. Even Martin Luther (1483–1546), who severely challenged the church otherwise, had his own way of questioning Copernicus' idea, apparently alluding to the biblical reference in which Joshua commanded the sun to stand still (Joshua 10:12–13).

Copernicus died shortly after he published this idea, therefore escaping serious censorship from the church. Johannes Kepler, who lived around one hundred years after Copernicus (1571–1630), built further on this new idea. He developed what came to be called the laws of planetary motion. Establishing himself as an astronomer and mathematician it was also significant that he was a German Protestant thus making it possible to avoid Roman church opposition. His contemporary, Galilei Galileo (1564–1642), having developed his own version of the newly invented telescope, furthered ideas of heliocentricity, and eventually earned a reputation as the father of modern science. At the time, however, Galileo's ideas were severely challenged by the Roman Church, because they appeared to contradict the clear teaching of the Bible (a geocentric interpretation of statements such as the one in Psalm 93:1).

As an aside, this development in thought, from a geocentric paradigm to a heliocentric one, is an iconic illustration of the perceived conflict that often seems to arise between faith and reason, or religion and science. In many ways, it represents an apparent clash of cultures, but it also demonstrates the delicate balance between a thorough understanding of God's special revelation (the Bible) and the commendable work of good research concerning the natural world. As many scholars have demonstrated over the years, the two need not be mutually exclusive. Many strongly professing Christians have shown that it's possible to retain a profound faith in the biblical revelation while still pursuing good scientific work.

Indeed, the Bible itself commends this kind of research. In chapters 38 to 41 of Job, for example, God shows Job that though there is much that may be impossible to know about the mysteries of his world, an inquiring education about these things is praiseworthy. It's part of the stewardship mandate that was given to humankind from the beginning, as demonstrated by Adam in his role of "naming the animals" (Genesis 2). In Proverbs 25:2, we read that while the glory of God is shrouded in mystery, it is the glory of kings to have an inquisitive mind about those mysteries.

There are many other biblical examples, including Joseph, Moses, and Daniel, as well as those like Saint Paul and Luke—leaders in the early church—who combined their "secular" knowledge with divine insight for good purposes. In 1 Chronicles 12:32, the men of Issachar are commended because, *"they understood the times and knew what Israel should do"* (NIV).

In this context, the Copernican story stands as a wonderful example of how the church must be careful about making assumptions and forming conclusions from the biblical texts that may not necessarily line up with reality. Since all truth is really God's truth, just because a discovery of some scientific reality does not take place in an explicitly Christian context doesn't mean it may be invalid. On the other hand, this example shows us that we need to take an approach to interpreting scripture that may often be quite out of sync with ill-tested scientific theories or popular culture. As we study the biblical revelation, we need to seek for a proper sense of spiritual and academic discernment to know when a paradigm shift is illusory or valid. I'll address this matter of scriptural hermeneutical integrity further in a subsequent chapter.

In any case, all historians readily acknowledge that around the dawn of the seventeenth century, as these new approaches and discoveries of science were taking place, a major philosophical shift was also occurring that radically affected the lifestyle and focus of Western culture for the next 350 years. We know it today as the Age of Reason, the Renaissance, and the Enlightenment. As illustrated above, this period, which came to be known as modernism, was characterized by a new kind of rationalism that seriously challenged previously held conventional ideas, especially those held by the church. One could say that a certain kind of rational pride or hubris began to emerge in the hearts and minds of people in this time. The idea of God being central to all that was happening in the world slowly gave way to the idea that humankind was supremely capable of universal knowledge and of taking responsibility for its own destiny. Science and the scientific method of inquiry became the new way of knowing. As a result, instead of God being the primary referent, man himself became the center of his own knowing.

Some of the better known philosophical contributors to the modern period have already been mentioned, but others also are worth noting.

Desiderius Erasmus (1466–1536): Though he lived as a priest in loyalty to the Roman Catholic Church near the end of medieval times, Erasmus raised questions that contributed towards church reforms and Reformation thinking. Because of his tendencies towards rationalism within the church context, he became known as the first of the Christian humanists.

Martin Luther (1483–1546): Perhaps influenced by men like Erasmus, Luther was a German theologian in the Roman Catholic Church who took critique of the church to a whole new level. Because he was critical of the church's promotion of indulgences (payment to the church for the forgiveness of sins), and because he affirmed the Bible as a more important authority than the church and emphasized salvation by grace through faith instead of works (all, for which, he suffered excommunication), he is largely known as the initiator of the Protestant Reformation as well as modern evangelicalism.

Baruch Spinoza (1623–1677): As a philosopher of Jewish and Portuguese descent, Spinoza also challenged conventional theological ideas, in this case those of his Jewish heritage. He postulated that God and nature were essentially the same and that morality was somewhat relative to circumstance and culture.

Gottfried Leibniz (1646–1716): A Christian German philosopher, Leibniz advanced ideas regarding the harmony of nature with the existence of God. He built upon the ideas of Aristotle regarding logic and contributed significantly to the development of mathematics, the principles of modern computerization, and physics.

This evolving shift yielded most profound implications. On the one hand, a new sense of freedom emerged that seriously questioned conventional ideas. Using the scientific method and other forms of logic, rationalism in every field of human endeavour became a new kind of interest. One of the benefits of this shift was that folk religion and superstitious ideas about life began to hold less influence. But a general sense of commitment to authentic biblical faith also took a big hit during this time, simply because of the emerging rationalism.

It should also be noted, of course, that one of the most significant developments of this period was the invention of the printing press in 1443 by the German, Johannes Gutenberg. Up to that time, all documents were painstakingly hand-written. It's also noteworthy that Gutenberg's main motivation for the pursuit of this invention was the more rapid multiplication of copies of the Bible so that many more people could read it for themselves. All of this contributed to a willingness to challenge existing notions, interpretations, and attitudes of church leaders. For many other reasons, it's not surprising that the invention of the printing press is highly regarded as the most important invention of the 2nd millennium.

With this background information, it's relatively simple to identify some of the main characteristics of the modern period, with which people of that period would be very familiar. One of the foundational assumptions in modernism is that it's possible to know the truth. In other words, truth exists independent of man's own existence, and with the right kind of methodological inquiry, it's possible to come to verifiable conclusions. Modernism relied heavily upon methodologies of inquiry, of which the scientific method was chief. The main tenet in modernism was that man was capable of discovering reality. It was just a matter of using a systematic approach in asking the right questions.

Modernism was the age of empiricism, in which it was presumed possible to understand reality based on experience and experimentation. In my own university education, I found that empiricism was a popular reference to scientific study. It spoke of finality and authority in coming to conclusions about reality. The word itself implies a kind of universal application about various ideas and conclusions. For that reason, modernism is often spoken of as foundationalism or evidentialism. It assumed that something is absolutely true based on diligent observation and careful examination. It emphasized objectivity, the concept that one could discover the existence of reality as something totally separate from mere opinion. The antithesis of objectivity, subjectivism, was presumed unreliable because it consisted of personal conjecture as opposed to scientific analysis.

Another important development in the modern period was that of structuralism. This simply meant that since absolute truth concerning all manner of things was assumed and discoverable (foundationalism), then it was possible to build or construct all kinds of applications upon that foundation. This resulted in a kind of absolutism during the modern period in which it was implied that the universe was established with a definite sense of order and design. Theologians, for example, were inclined to establish certainty about the existence of God based on well-researched evidences of design in various structures of nature—the human body, the rotation of the planets, and other natural phenomenon. This approach led to structured ways of thinking in which everything was related. In contrast to the idea of scattered and unrelated elements in the universe, modernism encouraged monolithic, or all-encompassing, ways of thinking. The world made sense because everything was contained within a closed system. From a theological perspective, the world had a beginning and an end. Within that system, Christianity provided an easily understood metanarrative, or overarching story of how the world was established, how it functioned, and where it was headed.

It is for this reason that some of the main features of the modern period concern this approach to life. There is, in the modern period, a huge emphasis on the importance of reason as a way of knowing. Reason itself came to affect every area of human interest and study.

Rationalism applied to science meant that with proper observation and careful measurement, one could discover why things were as they were. Based on those discoveries, one could make further discoveries and inventions. One of the most significant influences based on the rationalism of this period came out of Charles Darwin's theories about natural selection. These ideas were published in 1859 in his classic work entitled, *The Origin of the Species.* The book monumentally furthered the development of rationalism and effectively challenged existing theological and biblical ideas about divine creation. Ultimately, Darwin's ideas also contributed substantially to the development of postmodern thought because it raised questions about theological assumptions.

The modern period prevailed well into the latter part of the twentieth century. For those of us who were born and educated in the middle of the last century, modernism was still an important influence and default way of thinking. It was the underlying philosophy that set the stage for the nature of popular culture in which the emphasis was on order, structures of authority, and significant degrees of formality. Education at every level was geared to support this basic philosophical paradigm. Public education was structured to ensure a methodical approach to the integration of the various disciplines, including mathematics, science, history, English literature, and even art. Education itself, or the acquisition of educational degrees, was a way of recognizing authority.

For my purposes, I am especially interested in how modernism affected theological study and experience in the Christian church. My personal context happened to be evangelicalism, which developed within the Protestant tradition as a reaction to theological liberalism during the modern period. There is a sense in which theological liberalism itself developed as an extreme expression of rationalism in the modern period. It was led by such notables as Immanuel Kant, a German philosopher of the mid-to-late 1700s, who believed that reason was ultimately the basis for morality and ethics. Another very influential figure in theological liberalism was the German, Fredrick Schleiermacher (1768–1834). He concluded that humanity's inner spiritual feelings were reflections and responses to a greater spiritual reality.

From Saint Augustine to the Reformation, the intellectual aspects of Western civilization and the concept of truth were dominated by theologians. But beginning with the Renaissance period of the fourteenth to seventeenth centuries western civilization began to elevate scientific thinkers to the center of knowledge. If one were to look at human periods of history like a family tree, the Renaissance would be modernism's grandmother, and the Enlightenment would be its mother.

The Enlightenment was, in a way, the complete imposition of the scientific model of rationality upon all aspects of truth. It claimed that only scientific data could be objectively understood, defined, and defended. Truth, as it pertained to religion, was left out and discarded. It was Immanuel Kant in his work, *The Critique of Pure Reason*, appearing in 1781, that straddled this epoch's and postmodernism's contribution to relative truth. Among other things, Kant argued that true knowledge about God was impossible, so he created a divide of knowledge between "facts" and "faith." According to Kant, facts had nothing to do with religion. The result was that spiritual matters were assigned to matters of the heart and mere opinion; it was surmised that only the empirical sciences could speak of truth. And while modernism believed in absolutes at least in the matter of science, God's special revelation (the Bible) was essentially evicted from the realm of truth and certainty.

The outstanding characteristic of theological liberalism of the late modern period was the belief that a certain kind of rationalism was foundational to theological thought. This led to the idea of higher criticism relating to the biblical texts themselves, in which the Bible was analyzed according to the source and nature of the original texts. Higher criticism tended to challenge the idea of divine inspiration, focusing rather on the human origins of the biblical texts. Rudolf Bultmann of the late modern period (1887–1976) took biblical criticism to a new level when he proposed that the miraculous element in the Bible was simply a form of contextualized speaking and writing that had to be demythologized, or divested of its supernatural character.

Evangelicalism, one might say, rose as a reaction to this extreme form of rationalism. Some of it developed as a softer complement to the fundamentalist movement that came about in answer to theological liberalism. Concerned about the influence of liberal theology on sliding moral values, a variety of graduates from Princeton Seminary (including men like Gresham Machen and B. B. Warfield) in the early twentieth century wrote extensively about returning to "the fundamentals" of the Christian faith. These included a commitment to the inerrancy of scripture, the virgin birth and deity of Jesus Christ, his atoning death and resurrection for sin, and his literal bodily return to establish the Kingdom of God on earth.

Even before the days of modern fundamentalism, evangelical-ism gained prominence, especially under the influence of revival-ists such as John Wesley and George Whitefield of the eighteenth century. They took the Bible at face value as the very Word of God. Its stories and miracles, they believed, were not mere human con-coctions, but accurate representations of God's human connection and self-revelation. The Bible's purpose, evangelicals believed, was to reveal the nature of God's salvation in the life and work of Jesus Christ, which all could experience by a spiritual rebirth through faith in him.

This belief system resulted in a strong emphasis on the proc-lamation of the Good News, which developed into the major missionary movement of the modern period. For those of the late modern period, evangelicalism was probably best represented by the American evangelist Billy Graham. He came to be known best for his "crusades," which consisted of large city, stadium-filled events throughout America and the world from about 1947 to 2005. In these large events, he preached about the need to respond, through a very specific act of confessing faith, to the truth of the gospel of God's salvation in Jesus Christ.

It's important to note that evangelicalism itself was also greatly influenced by the rationalism of the modern period. The very notion of systematic theology, for example, illustrates a more ratio-nal approach to biblical understanding and application. Evangelical seminaries of the modern period, such as Dallas Theological Seminary, Trinity Evangelical Divinity School, and Fuller Theological Seminary, specialized in various forms of structured theological and mission-related thinking. This systematization involved a kind of scriptural analysis that resulted in the develop-ment of diverse theological ideas and the formation of a myriad of Christian church denominations within the Protestant tradition.

Among them were differences of theological opinion respecting such matters as ecclesiology (church government), eschatology (prophecies related to Jesus' second coming), or pneumatology (the ministry of the Holy Spirit).

For seminary students such as myself at Canadian Theological Seminary in Regina, Saskatchewan (now Ambrose University in Calgary, Alberta) from 1970 to 1972, attention was given to the study of the Bible in terms of systems of theological thought as well as ministry methods peculiar to our evangelical, denominational heritage. Homiletics, for example, emphasized the need to preach in a manner that systematically exegeted the biblical text according to certain prescribed rules of hermeneutics, while also paying attention to effective means of elocution or delivery, as well as personal application. Likewise, pastoral theology was geared to focus on methods of pastoral ministry, including such things as pastoral counselling, the proper form of conducting Christian rites of passage (baptisms, weddings, funerals), and the best methods of church administration.

In summary, the modern period was a time of extreme rationalism applied to all manner of life's responsibilities and challenges, including Christian thought, Christian experience and church ministry. Of course, this emphasis on reason should not be considered totally unbiblical. After all, thought processes are an essential part of our human existence. The Bible itself consists of many examples by all its writers of rational arguments for conclusions and the development of various doctrines. Consider, for example, the instance of Saint Paul's argument for salvation by faith alone in Romans 4.

The biggest problem apart from the extreme rationalism of this period was the development of a kind of human hubris that gave people a sense of optimism and control over their own lives and destiny. In the context of Christianity and church ministry, rationalism prevailed to the point of what often appeared to be mere human approaches to analysis at the expense of more spiritual ways of gaining insight and understanding. In the process, the importance of prayer and other means of spiritual discernment were given less emphasis than various academic approaches to life and ministry. As we shall see, it could be argued in postmodernism that the pendulum has swung to the other extreme.

The other effect of modernism on the Christian church was the development of a kind of snobbish attitude about its own importance in relation to other points of view. Instead of generating humility based on the Christian view of the meaning of grace, sometimes Christians were prone to convey an air of superiority towards those of other belief systems. There are many instances in which this criticism was undoubtedly justified, but as we shall see, this sense of superiority is something of which postmoderns have also been guilty, not recognizing their own tendencies to the same.

Postmodernism

There is an important sense in which the development of philosophical thought is part of an historical continuum in which the various parts are not as distinct as we imagine or describe them to be. For example, there surely were signs of modernism's rationalism even during what we would ordinarily think of as the premodern period. And certainly, this is also true of the perceived transition between modernism and postmodernism. In fact, some suggest that the postmodernism of which we speak is merely an extension of the old modernism, since it appears to have taken rationalism to a new extreme level.

Surely it must be granted that there is some overlap so that it may be proper to speak of postmodernism, as some have done, as *modernity*. However, I believe it's quite possible to show that postmodernism is a more distinct development, within a broader modernity, that has come about since about the middle of the twentieth century.

In speaking of the origins of postmodern thinking, where does one begin? No doubt there are a variety of opinions based on different perspectives. It's probably fair to say that there is no precise explanation about the origins of postmodernism, but there are a variety of influences that ultimately led to the rejection of rationalism which so obviously characterized the modern period. At the very least, it is evident from what is observed in popular culture that Western society is no longer governed by the same philosophical ideas that prevailed earlier. Something has dramatically changed, and the change is much more revolutionary than we might imagine!

It is generally acknowledged by students of philosophy that the seeds of postmodernity were sown by the philosophical thinking of people like Immanuel Kant and Frederick Nietzsche. Immanuel Kant, as mentioned earlier, believed that conceptions of reality were impositions of our own thought processes rather than the other way around (as implied in Christian thought). In other words, the structures of reality that we'd assumed were ordained by God, in his mind were simply products of human ways of thinking rather than representations of reality. In that sense, the world was actually unknowable.

Whereas Kant marked the philosophical transition from the Enlightenment to modernism, Frederick Nietzsche may symbolize the shift from modernism to postmodernism. As the "patron saint" of postmodernist philosophy, Nietzsche held to "perspectivism," which theorizes that all knowledge (including science) is a matter of perspective and interpretation. Nietzsche, who lived more than a hundred years after Kant, furthered the latter's idea in the form of an emphasis on self-actualization in which people think more in terms of responsibility for their own existence and destiny. Nietzsche is "credited" with the idea that God is dead, and that God is a construct of the human mind in a way that isn't relevant to human reality. It was Nietzsche who invented the idea of "nihilism," or the denial of a reason or cause for human existence, so that we should not expect to find meaning in life. These ideas also fit well with the evolutionary ideas of Charles Darwin, Nietzsche's contemporary, who concluded that the development of life as we know it was a result of survival through self-determination.

In the mid-twentieth century, Christian philosopher Francis Schaeffer wrote extensively about the implications of this denial of rational thought in his book, *Escape from Reason*. In doing so, he anticipated some of the basic tenets of postmodernism, which essentially denies the modernist idea of logical thought processes. Schaeffer wrote broadly abut existentialism, a term first used by the Danish Lutheran pastor Søren Kierkegaard. Existentialism emphasizes the importance of the subjective experience as the most valid expression of truth. Kierkegaard elevated the idea of faith and passion for its own sake. It was he who spoke in terms of "a leap of faith," meaning that the experience of faith was more important than the object in which faith is placed, since we can't be sure of any objective reality. Miriam-Webster's dictionary defines existentialism as:

> ... a chiefly 20th century philosophical movement embracing diverse doctrines but centering on analysis of individual existence in an

unfathomable universe and the plight of the
individual who must assume ultimate responsibility for acts of free will without any certain knowledge of what is right or wrong or good or bad.[10]

A couple of other key figures in the early development of
postmodern thought were Martin Heidegger (1889–1976) and
Jean-Paul Sartre (1905–1980). Heidegger felt that in contrast to
rational thought, the most important idea was a person's existence
in relation to other things. He emphasized the idea of authenticity—one's own experience in relation to his or her place in life—
and the importance of words, subjectively so, as symbols of one's
own reality. Jean-Paul Sartre, on the other hand, is best known
for his denial of any meaning to life because of the final reality of
death for every living thing. In his view, we are only able to make
something out of our existence through the freedom of choice.
In other words, our existence is defined by our choices, which we
must make because they are thrust upon us. We define humanity by
the choices we make.

It is easy to see how these philosophical influences began to
shape the culture of Western society to move it beyond the modern
period. In a sense, postmodernism came to represent a more radical
form of rationalism that reduced reality to individual choice. In a
simplified way, it transitioned Western thought from the idea of
man as the center of reality to the idea of "the self" at the center. In
his book, *Fools Talk: The Art of Christian Persuasion*, Os Guinness,
the contemporary English writer and social critic, quaintly

---

10   By permission. From Merriam-Webster's Collegiate® Dictionary, 11th
     Edition ©2017, Accessed January 2, 2017, https://www.merriam-
     webster.com/dictionary/existentialism.

describes this shift. He calls it, "the age of the self and the selfie." Because these developments also happened at a time of technical advance using the Internet, in contrast to the dictum of the modern period ("I think, therefore I am"), he expresses the one for this age as, "I post; therefore, I am!"[11]

One of the outcomes of these twentieth century philosophical developments was the reduction of reality to one's individual existence and identity through various forms of self-expression. Two figures that had a profound influence on postmodern thought were Michael Foucault (1926–1984) and Jacques Derrida (1930–2004). Foucault believed that life is all about power, most often used quite unconsciously. Derrida combined Foucault's idea of power with the further idea that words were merely extensions of our individual conceptions of reality. Thus, he believed that words needed to be deconstructed in terms of their intended meaning versus their apparent meaning. In other words, since you couldn't depend on words to convey any precise meaning, they needed to be analyzed in terms of their tendency to manipulate.

One other significant figure in the development of postmodernism was Jean Francois Lyotard (1924–1988), a contemporary of Foucault and Derrida. He suggested that reality cannot be explained in terms of any one big story. Instead, the world needed to recognize the diversity of micro-stories that characterized various people's traditions. He became famous for being anti-metanarrative -- opposing any thought of a grand narrative, including the Christian one.

---

11   Os Guinness, *Fools Talk: The Art of Christian Persuasion* (Downers Grove, Ill: InterVarsity Press, 2015), 15.

What has been presented in this brief outline is a mere summary of some of the main ideas that began to prevail in the twentieth century. Obviously, there is much more that could be said about the ideas and influence of various thinkers of this period, but the point is that these ideas began to coalesce into a series of common notions that have influenced contemporary culture. The main philosophical ideas of the postmodern period concern the importance of self-expression in any particular case. It's important to recognize that, from this perspective, life and human history cannot be explained in terms of any specific story or narrative. In that way, postmodernism is completely anti-metanarrative. As a result, it is up to individuals, families, and various social groups to develop their own stories.

I suppose it could easily be a matter of debate whether philosophical ideas came first or merely began to mirror what was already reflected in the popular culture of the time. More likely than not, they developed together. Those who think philosophically are not necessarily interested in, or take responsibility for, generating popular cultural trends. If anything, they observe trends in human thinking and behaviour and simply try to describe what they perceive in philosophical terms. On the other hand, their ideas gain recognition and serve to promote trends in the culture, so there is a sense in which they develop together. Philosophical ideas simply give voice to the emergence of certain cultural practices.

At the same time, it is evident that the influence of postmodern thinking on popular culture is expansive and profound. Whether we recognize it or not, all of us (including those of us who identify ourselves as Christians) have been deeply affected by these developments, especially those of us who belong to a younger generation. Keeping this in mind, it may be helpful to enumerate some of the main features of postmodernism as it exists in popular culture at this time.

CHAPTER 5

Prevailing Features
of Postmodernism

For many readers, the following list of postmodern characteristics will not be entirely new, and undoubtedly there are a variety of descriptions and classifications by which these might be presented or discussed. These descriptions represent my own understanding and perspective of some of the most outstanding outcomes of postmodern thinking, arranged in some measure of priority (from a modern perspective). At the very least, such a list, in certain contexts, might provide the opportunity for further discussion and application.

Epistemology

It may be a "modern" idea, but sooner or later all of us are inclined to ask the question about how we know what we know (or think we know). This is the essence of philosophical inquiry. In the modern period, knowledge of anything was based on the idea that there was such a thing as objective reality that could be understood through careful observation and conclusions. Objective truth is the idea that something exists apart from any human perception of it. It is the idea that if a tree falls in the forest, it will still make a sound, even if no one is around to hear it.

The best way to know anything, it was thought during the modern period, was to apply the elements of the scientific method—observation, hypothesis, testing, analysis, and conclusion. The scientific method was the way to proceed concerning any inquiry towards knowledge, especially if it had to do with the natural world. Some form of this kind of inquiry was basic to every other form of knowledge, including the social sciences of psychology and sociology, as well as studies in history, theology, and the practice of law. It also was the means by which to acquire technical and practical skills of every kind, including those related to business, government, and various trades.

But in postmodernism, the very notion of objective reality is no longer taken very seriously. Instead, knowledge of anything is a very personal thing. It is individualized, or merely common to certain groups of people with a purpose peculiar to their own making. Therefore, even though the scientific method is still employed for practical reasons, it no longer seems to hold the esteem it once did. For one thing, the thinking goes, one can't necessarily trust that the conclusions of the scientific method are completely reliable, or that they will serve one's best purposes. As well, so-called science, as is apparent in various political debates, can be used to bolster one's own position on any particular matter.

That is why, for example, there is so much debate regarding climate change. Scientific conclusions, it seems are not consistent, or are used to strengthen differences of opinion based on philosophical, religious, and political grounds.

From the postmodern perspective, objective truth doesn't really exist; knowledge, at best, is a matter of one's own understanding, and worse still, used for one's own agenda to control others. In the end, knowledge is peculiar to one's own experience, which may be acquired in a large variety of ways, including such means as parapsychology, social interaction or religious experiences.

History

One of the effects of postmodernism is best illustrated by questions that have emerged regarding historical documents. History is obviously written from the perspective of the writer, and is thus a matter of personal interpretation. It's been said, for example, that history is written by the victors, meaning that it tends to have a distinct bias that undoubtedly will differ from the facts, or certainly from the perspective of the victims. A classic example of this, with various interpretations, concerns the cause and outcomes of the world wars. It's been argued by some, for example, that the Jewish Holocaust was exaggerated by those who are sympathetic to Zionism. Though we may vehemently disagree with this interpretation, the point is that one's personal perspective radically influences their conclusion.

It is important to understand that postmodernism essentially denies the existence of truth in any form, because reality is merely something created in the mind of each person. In that sense, there is no such thing as true history, because all of it is a matter of someone's personal interpretation. In the mind of the postmodern person, we each create our own history, or story, and there really is no point in trying to see a pattern in the events of others in our lives. Granted, this is an extreme expression of a postmodern view of history but in actual postmodern experience, it is thought, any rendition of an historical event is subject to someone's peculiar perspective. Historical accounts of any kind need to be deconstructed to determine the nature of the motive or power being represented. Thus, rather than a focus on historical fact (common to those who think from a modern perspective), the postmodern emphasis is on trying to discern the motivation of power.

The implications of this perspective on culture in general, and on Christianity in particular, are most profound. Rather than looking at the Bible as an historical document, the postmodernist is inclined to suspect that every part of it was written to promote a peculiar agenda. Accordingly, to the typical postmodernist, the Bible's accounts of what actually happened must be deconstructed. The meaning of the words in those accounts cannot be taken at face value, because no one is able to know what the words actually meant. This same suspicion applies to a lot of documentation that has to do with the history of the church.

As has been said, this represents an extreme view of postmodernism's engagement with history, yet it is not uncommon for today's typical millennial to be somewhat distrustful of any pretension of authentic historical fact. Always there is the question of what the motive or orientation might be of the one who is representing a certain subject or account. Thus, in postmodernism, it seems that *fact* has given way to *opinion*.

Pluralism

I owe much of my understanding of the development of postmodernism to Dr. Donald Carson, a research professor of New Testament at Trinity Evangelical Divinity School in Deerfield, Illinois. In his book, *The Gagging of God*, Carson differentiates between various kinds of pluralism, which he categorizes as empirical pluralism, cherished pluralism, and philosophical or hermeneutical pluralism.[12] By empirical pluralism, Carson means how it is evident in the culture of our times that there are many different ideas about God and spirituality, which are all considered equally valid. This is the essence of pluralism. In fact, this means that Christianity no longer holds the primary position of religious respect in our country, or in the Western world. The statistical decline in church participation and attendance reflects this reality.

By cherished pluralism, Carson refers to what society has come to accept as normal and beneficent. It means that what anyone chooses to believe is entirely up to each individual and should be admired, not merely accepted. This idea is essentially an extension of cultural pluralism.

But it is philosophical pluralism that represents the greatest challenge to Christianity and the church of these times. It means that pluralism is now entrenched as the dominant philosophy of our times respecting differences of ideas on religion and spirituality. In fact, it is now considered a moral transgression or injustice to think of one religious idea as better or superior to another. Perhaps more than any other aspect of modern culture, this change illustrates the profound relationship between philosophical and cultural developments. The implication once again, especially for Christianity and the church, is large. Because of the very nature of the gospel message and the claims of Jesus Christ himself, Christians have always understood that message to be unique. For this reason, pluralism represents a special challenge for Christian ministry, which has been more recently addressed in a variety of ways (the subject of a subsequent chapter).

---

12 Don Carson, *The Gagging of God: Christianity Confronts Pluralism* (Grand Rapids, MI: Zondervan, 1996), 13.

Tolerance

As I write today, I am thinking of a recent editorial in the local newspaper in which a local Christian children's ministry is being critiqued because its staff and volunteers are asked to sign a statement regarding their commitment to a standard of sexual conduct that conforms to the ministry's basic beliefs. Citing biblical references about not judging others, this writer uses the word "tolerance" to describe the attitude leaders should have towards those who challenge the biblical standard that has been set.[13]

Drawing on the heart of pluralism, the "t-word," as I call it, is one of the most critical elements in postmodernism. Since the validity of anyone's perspective is a matter of opinion, and any judgement of that opinion must be considered a way of "taking advantage" of the other person, then such an attitude must be seen as intolerant, which in the minds of the postmodern age is the worst kind of travesty. In the postmodern way of thinking, tolerance is king -- or at least one of the most important values to hold. It is said that we must be careful to be tolerant of every opinion except, of course, intolerance! Anyone who isn't tolerant is regarded as a bigot, or worse still, one who discriminates in a negative way towards other people. Hence, the concern about the development of attitudes that might easily be interpreted as racist.

Tolerance is at the heart of the Charter of Rights and Freedoms. In Canada, the Charter says that:

> ... every individual is equal before and under the law and has the right to the equal protection and

---

13   Neil Godbout, "Editorial: Words to Live By," *Prince George Citizen* (Prince George, BC), July 22, 2016.

equal benefit of the law without discrimination and, in particular, without discrimination based on race, national or ethnic origin, colour, religion, sex, age or mental or physical disability.[14]

Under the Human Rights Act in Canada, there are eleven different areas of potential discrimination. They are:

- race
- national or ethnic origin
- colour
- religion
- age
- sex
- sexual orientation
- marital status
- family status
- disability
- a conviction for which a pardon has been granted or a record suspended[15]

I shall discuss the merits of this concept later in the context of Christian service, but it's worth noting the tremendous importance of tolerance in postmodern thought. Its development is a natural outcome of a philosophy that denies the existence of objective truth as a metanarrative or all-encompassing worldview. Of special

---

14 "Constitution Act 1982, Part I, Canadian Charter of Rights and Freedoms," *Justice Laws Website, Government of Canada*, accessed January 2, 2017, http://laws-lois.justice.gc.ca/eng/Const/page-15.html.

15 "Grounds of Discrimination," *Human Rights Complaints*, Government of Canada. Accessed January 2, 2017, http://www.canada.pch.gc.ca/eng/1448633333941/1448633333943#a2a.

significance to Christianity, the idea of tolerance consistently challenges any sense of superior knowledge or insight, because such
would imply some measure of social power.
A corollary of tolerance is the notion of judgement. Ironically,
this is an area in which the postmodernist will often appeal to the
biblical account of Jesus' condemnation of self-righteous judgement (demonstrated by the Pharisees of his time), as was done in
the editorial illustration cited above. Quoting extensively from the
Gospels (Luke 6:37, Matthew 7:3, among other references), the
editor writes:

> Christ was tolerant of many things, but clearly
> self-righteousness was not one of them. If His
> own words are any indication, Jesus would have
> had little patience for the self-righteous tone of
> the [Christian ministry's] code of conduct.[16]

It is not uncommon for those who sometimes protest or express
a contrary opinion to be labelled as bigots or racists. For example,
homosexuality is now accepted as a legitimate lifestyle, and those
who have a different perspective on this preference are commonly
referred to as "homophobic." As there is also wide acceptance of
homosexuality as a genetically-based issue (something not actually indisputably established in any objective way), those who
beg to differ are often referred to as "racist." Ironically, that kind
of reverse discrimination is happening frequently—those who
express doubt or a differing point-of-view are maligned. This is
one of the challenges of living in a postmodern world.

---

16   Neil Godbout, Ibid.

Deification of the "Self"

I referred earlier to Os Guinness' characterization of the post-modern era as the age of the "self and the selfie!" This is a very apt description. Since postmodernism has abandoned the notion of truth, the absolute, the metanarrative, and the existence of a transcendent God, everyone is presumably free to create their own reality. This is now happening in a variety of ways. For example, in the context of the recent proliferation of "new age" religion and in reference to another writer (Peter Jones, *The Gnostic Empire Strikes Back*, 1992), Carson writes:

> The aim is not to be reconciled to a transcendent God, who has made us and against whom we have rebelled, but to grow in self-awareness and self-fulfillment, to become self-actualized, to grow to our full potential, until we are rather more at one with the god/universe than we otherwise would be.[17]

There are various outcomes of this new attitude towards religion. One is a complete rejection of all forms of traditional religion. The idea in postmodern thinking on one hand is that religion is not something that should be institutionalized; it is, after all, a very individual matter. Besides, institutionalism, according to postmodernism, is a relic of the modern period. Religion, the postmodernist would say, needs to be deconstructed. Thus, it is not uncommon to see many examples of millennials and Gen-Xers who have left the church and organized religion for a more

---

17   Carson, *The Gagging of God*, 41.

individualized spirituality. Tim Keller cites statistics and speaks of these kinds of people as "nones."[18] Often, they are inclined to seek a religious experience, for example, in nature, in an artistic form, in some aspect of oriental religion, in sexual experimentation, or in the use of mind-altering drugs.

Another response to traditional religion among postmodernists is syncretism—the mixing of various religious ideas and practices to focus on common patterns of religious expression. This week someone passed on a fairly recent book of interest along these lines entitled, *In Praise of Mixed Religion*. In it, the author writes that syncretism is often regarded negatively because it "... describes the process of mixing and matching bits from more than one religion."[19] In the Introduction, he quips, "We have a habit... of seeing clarity and simplicity where there is really only messy complexity. The discussion about syncretism is a way of pointing to this complexity."[20]

One should take note here of the references to messiness and complexity—allusions to the philosophical chaos that characterizes postmodernism. Syncretism is attractive in these times because it is a way of resolving the dogmatism of religious discourse so typical of the modern age. It also aids in fostering an attitude of tolerance spoken of earlier. Postmodernists like the idea of syncretism because it challenges traditional notions of religion. Through

---

18   Tim Keller, *Center Church: Doing Balanced, Gospel-Centered Ministry in Your City* (Grand Rapids: Zondervan, 2012), 184.

19   William Harrison, *In Praise of Mixed Religion; The Syncretism Solution in a Multifaith World* (Montreal: McGill-Queen's University Press, 2014), 8.

20   Harrison, xiv.

syncretism, one can choose what's suitable according to one's own judgement of what may or may not be important.

As described earlier, one of the outstanding characteristics of postmodernism is the importance of the self—many would say to the point of deification—which is why it is appropriate to speak of it in the context of religion. Whereas we might think of the pre-modern period as more or less having God at the center of all things, in the sense that he was the primary reference for life, and modernism placing Man at the center of his own knowing, postmodernism quite explicitly tends to put Self at the center. I know these generalizations may seem simplistic but according to the main thesis of this book, it is evident that there has been a shift over time in this direction. This shift should not be surprising, since a self-centered conclusion is the natural outcome of man-centered thinking.

If you think about it, self-expression is one of the most important elements in today's Western culture, and the advance of technology has contributed significantly to this development. In fact, technology itself has become a bit of an obsession for the typical postmodern person, simply because it enables people to express themselves with a good sense of personal power. I know this seems somewhat ironic, since there is an element in postmodernism that seriously disparages the advancement of technology and its effects. Jacques Ellul, for example, an influential French philosopher of the last century and favoured thinker among postmodernists, made a lot out of the possible tyranny of technology. Yet the development of technology has played a large role in the proliferation of personal expression through the arts. Consider, for example, the number of people who seek to express themselves through music and video these days. This is the case in every instance of current artistic expression—theatre, cinema, television, pop concerts, dance, paint, and verbal communication.

Though it is evident that the daily newspaper has grown to be a less popular and effective medium of communication, written communication still flourishes in many other ways—not only through publications and personal blogs on the Internet, but also through books, of which this one is an example. My own interest in writing started, in part, with the opportunity to develop a personal Internet website and blog, which now includes almost 300 articles.[21]

It seems rather strange that in a time when the main medium of communication is switching from print to the Web, the publication of books is actually increasing. This is simply because increasing numbers of people are able to access vast quantities of information more easily while also publishing their thoughts more quickly. While the publishing industry has grown exponentially in recent years, it is likely more difficult to sell books simply because there are so many competing publications, not to mention Internet medium interests; however, the point is that the world has become much more prolific in expressing its thoughts and ideas on just about every subject. If there is one thing that describes these postmodern times, it is the technological development of computerization and the emergence of the Information Age.

The biggest development in the area of personal audio-visual expression is social media. It is quite unusual these days, at least in the West, to find someone who does not have a personal connection to the Internet, and thus also to social media. While many may be inclined to disparage full participation because of how these services tend to exploit people's privacy, social media continues to be increasingly popular, simply because it offers so much personal power in such a large variety of artistic expressions. It provides

---

21   http://www.secondwindministries.ca.

a means of control and influence not available in the past. Even though any given technical device may be morally neutral, social media can be used both for great good or great evil. Again, the popularity of social media in these times illustrates, perhaps better than anything else, the prominence of self-identity, personal power, and self-expression.

Many other forms of self-expression exist in these postmodern times. Consider the myriad of eclectic personal expressions that are made by individuals these days. Although there are definite style patterns in personal grooming for men and women, in a homogenous group of a dozen people, there may easily be as many radically different hairstyles. This is even true among professional athletes. My wife has a special interest in professional baseball, especially the Toronto Blue Jays! Because of her, I enjoy a good deal of exposure to these baseball games as well. If you have occasion to watch games in Major League Baseball, you will observe that some players are clean-shaven and more traditional in their appearance, while others sport beards, long hair, mullets, or any number of eclectic expressions of grooming. The variety in today's hairstyles is testimony in some small way, I believe, to this interest in self-expression.

There's also the matter of body markings/art, or tattoos. In the modern period, tattoos were the domain of the socially deviant. In that earlier period, tattoo inscriptions were rare, because they were not considered a matter of good taste and professionalism. Those who displayed tattoos were often marked as rebels in more ways than one. Today, however, it's almost unusual to find someone, especially among millennials, who does not have some kind of tattoo.

The case of tattoos is also a great example of a change of attitude that has taken place among the people of the Christian church.

In the modern era, such markings (as well as men wearing earrings or other body piercings) were considered a transgression of God's specific prohibition not to mark one's body (Leviticus 19:28). This was so, it is said, because it was important for God's people in that time to distinguish themselves from the pagan peoples among whom they lived. So, what's changed? The postmodern answer might be that such an interpretation of Leviticus is quite narrow, and that the prohibition was confined to the people of God in that time and place. Also, there is no New Testament equivalent to this prohibition in the Old Testament. Since Christians are now living under the new covenant of grace, they should be free to express their personalities, and even some Christian message, by this means. Besides, there seem to be other biblical references that could be regarded as encouraging this kind of thing, such as the one in Isaiah 49:16 about God inscribing his people on the palms of his hands, or being placed upon one's heart as a seal, "...*like a seal on your arm*" (Song of Solomon 8:6, NIV).

Nevertheless, even in a postmodern context, some Christians would likely advise careful thought about this kind of liberty, perhaps citing the Leviticus reference as a principle of Christian decorum. This illustration demonstrates how reasoning has changed from a stricter (modern) interpretation of the Bible to one that is less rigid. More significantly, since tattooing is now so prolific, even among those who were raised as "moderns," the matter is another vivid example of the importance of individualized personal expression in these postmodern times.

Non-hierarchical

One of the features of the modern era was a hierarchical model of leadership in government, business, and the church. It was especially apparent in the business of military organization. Modernists often reflected a militaristic approach to life and business management. That period represented social management using conferred authority and the power that came with it. In that structure, role positions and titles were quite important. In "modern" ways of thinking the world was ordered by certain prescribed patterns of structure; thus, it was only natural to also think of social relationships in this way. The existence of God may not have figured prominently in that structure, depending on one's views about religious matters. Nevertheless, one could say that an important feature of the modern period was order and structure *even in relationships.*

In his book, *Postmodern Times,* Gene Veith of Concordia University refers to the American architectural theorist, Charles Jencks, who believed that modernism came to an end at 3:32 p.m. on July 15, 1972.[22] How could he be so specific? Well, that was the moment in time when the Pruitt-Igoe government housing development in St. Louis, Missouri was demolished by dynamite. Veith writes,

> ... that though it was a pinnacle of modernist architecture [featuring] modernistic aesthetic and functional design, the project was impersonal and depressing ... The demolition of the Pruitt-Igoe development is a paradigm for postmodernism.

---

22 Gene Veith, *Postmodern Times: A Contemporary Guide to Thought and Culture* (Wheaton, Ill: Crossway Books, 2014), 39.

> The modern worldview constructs rationally designed systems in which human beings find it impossible to live.[23]

This illustration sums up the effect of postmodernism. Since it professes that there is no such thing as objective truth, no overarching story of explanation for the world's existence, no knowable origin or destiny for human existence, then there is no reason for any accountability—except to oneself. Postmodernism is intrinsically anti-authoritarian, anti-structuralist, and anti-hierarchical. The initial expressions of these were especially prominent in the widespread rejection of authority displayed during the 1960s. Those were the days of revolution and rebellion against the structures of capitalism and materialism, but in reality, the cultural upheaval of the sixties was the outcome of the spirit of postmodernism philosophically established earlier.

One way in which this attitude continues to prevail is in the ongoing reaction to authority as it exists in every form. Leadership today, typically looks a lot different than it once did. Postmodernism has effectively levelled the playing field. Autocratic leadership in any form is out; participatory leadership is in. In today's world, leaders are not recognized for their position, or even necessarily for their credentials. The true test of leaders today is whether they can engage others in the pursuit of values and goals that have been developed through collaboration and teamwork. As we shall see, this has great implications for the nature of pastoral leadership.

Speaking of leadership and authoritarianism in the context of the church, Frost and Hirsch propose that the church of today must distance itself from the hierarchical model of the past. Referring

---

23   Ibid.

to one example of pastoral leadership, they write, "...he has had to completely flatten his organization's leadership style."[24] This means that structures of leadership and authority are no longer the driving force in organizational development and structure.

Another way to think of this cultural change concerns the new emphasis on egalitarianism. Though often used in the church as a reference to the relationship between men and women in marriage or church ministry, the term has come to have a more general meaning that stresses the equal value of people in every context. Distinctions based on individual abilities and artistic expressions of every sort are one thing, but the intrinsic value of each person is quite another. It is this theme of equality that now has a huge bearing on the way people function in relation to one another in their homes, their places of work, and all their social relationships -- at least on the surface of things. Of course, the Christian response to the egalitarian emphasis, of which more will be written later, might well be that while all people are created with equal value, all are not necessarily endowed with the same resources, privileges, and opportunities. Besides, while the Bible supports the concept of equality in an expression like the "priesthood of all believers" (i.e. 1 Peter 2:9), it also is explicit about roles of submission and authority in relation in certain relationships (i.e. Ephesians 5:22-6:9; Colossians 3:18-25).

The result of this paradigm shift is a much softer approach to communication of every kind. Since no one has the last word on anything, persuasion is less coercive and less authoritarian in nature; it's actually more invitational. It is the language of "we" instead of "you." Today's parents (at least in public) are more

---

24   Frost and Hirsch, 21.

inclined to reason with their children, to make "suggestions" rather than "demands." There is less of an apparent age gap between those who are younger and those who are older. Older people seek to identify with their younger children in styles of dress, while the younger generation has abandoned formal means of addressing their "older peers," often referring to them (sometimes even their own parents) by their first names.

Successful leaders will emphasize a team approach to decision-making, rather than an authoritarian kind of approach. Work relationships will involve more light-hearted social interaction even in the context of more serious business decisions. Effective leaders want to be known for fostering a positive workplace environment so that workers are intrinsically, not extrinsically, motivated. They want people to have a sense of ownership over direction and decisions.

In a way, this participatory approach makes the task of leadership more challenging, because in a postmodern environment, people are more likely to respond to recognition and appreciation rather than to position and authority. Persuasion in any postmodern context is based more on an emotional sense of care instead of knowledge. A relevant quote attributed to Theodore Roosevelt says, "People don't care how much you know until they know how much you care."

This latter reference raises another important matter related to structure and communication among postmodernists—that emotional engagements are much more important than cognitive ones. This is actually a good way to understand the difference between the two paradigms. To understand the anti-dogma approach that is characteristic of postmodernists, it helps to also appreciate why they are more responsive to emotional appeals than to structured knowledge appeals. Often, they will comment in some way on the tendency of moderns and their knowledge-based presentations to illicit boredom.

Anti-structuralism fits with the idea that postmodernists aren't interested in linear thought patterns. I first encountered this with a younger associate, who said that being raised in a non-Western culture made him more inclined to circular or disconnected ways of thinking when organizing his thoughts. I didn't recognize it at the time, but in part he was reacting to my modern monolithic way of thinking. He had an emotional way of viewing pastoral ministry issues, whereas I thought of them more in logical terms. At the time, probably neither of us understood that we were the product of the times and places in which we had been raised. And the worst thing one might say in these times is that one is better than the other.

Experience

In the modern period, experience involved the idea of humankind taking responsibility to understand the world through the process of the scientific method. Empiricism, as this approach came to be called, had the rather narrow meaning of knowing the world through a prescribed (structured) kind of experimentation. As mentioned earlier, this was a notable distinction in knowing, compared with the importance of the God-centered, revelatory way of knowing in the pre-modern period. Empiricism, in that sense, was about objective experience.

In the postmodern way of thinking, experience is a very subjective thing, and fully represents the new way of knowing. Furthermore, subjective experience becomes the new means of judging whether something is true and right or not. Personal experience is the new authority. In the extreme, it means that everyone has the right to come to their own conclusions about reality, and all need to be respected for their own sake. This development is the natural outcome of the shift that has taken place towards a more self-centered kind of modernism.

In general, it is evident that personal experience has been promoted to a new level of importance in our daily lives. In many ways, the role of story or narrative trumps more analytical and structured ways of learning. In this kind of environment, giving people a chance to tell their story is the new priority. We tend to be much more sensitive to personal accounts, as illustrated by the growing importance of story in various news items. Front page attention, at least in our city, is now given to someone's personal experience, whereas previously such matters would have been relegated to the back pages of the newspaper. This is also often the case with television news. People seem to have an insatiable appetite for knowledge about the more intimate experiences of other people. This appears to be a departure from more traditional journalism, in which the big stories had to do with matters of business, politics, and crime.

Story is also a way of characterizing the subject of social relationships. People are more inclined to share candidly about their personal lives, even with mere acquaintances. Along with this phenomenon is the fact that there seems to be less of a stigma associated with sharing personal problems or failures. The sharing of personal story is not only a way of self-actualization in the telling, but also a means of self-identification in the listening. This reality has turned the tide in cinema and the television industry. It is the explanation behind the growing interest in reality television. Today, we want insight into the lives of real people with whom we can identify. We want to see how they live in the wilderness, how they date and marry, how they negotiate the challenges of business, work, and suffering.

This emphasis on experience and story has also been greatly enhanced by the development of social media. It is there that everyone can share their own personal experiences, and that recipients of those messages have the equal opportunity not only to see what is happening in the lives of their friends, but also to approve ("like") or give some other (emotive) personal response. Hence, the rise of the "emoji," something we never heard about in the modern era. Facebook is especially popular as a medium of storytelling. It is also a place where you can easily register your personal opinion, and therefore influence outcomes. Instead of judging a behaviour or political action based on some objective criterion or outside authority, it's simply a matter of seeing what the majority of one's friends are thinking. Friendship, especially by these means, is the new basis of decision making. Again, the implications, both for society in general and the church in particular, are extensive and profound.

There are many other expressions of this emphasis on experience, such as the apparent desire of millennials to out-do each other by their participation in experiences that are unusual or extreme. An anecdotal illustration (itself a postmodern method of communication) concerns my own experience several years ago during downhill skiing season while doing some work in Golden, BC. The lift itself, Kicking Horse Ski Resort, is known for having one of the highest verticals in Canada. Thankfully for my sake, and despite the slope's challenge and excitement, there were some gentler means of descent from the top of the mountain. But I was blown away by the kinds of extreme, almost vertical, slopes some of the skiers were successfully negotiating. In some cases, skiers were climbing way beyond the top of the gondola ski-lift to ply their skill in what appeared to be sheer verticals of several hundred meters. This exercise is commonly referred to as cliff-jumping. Perhaps this wasn't really new, but it does seem that among today's millennials there is a new interest, at least from my perspective, in extreme adventure.

This interest in risky living, I believe, is an extension of the general postmodern feeling that since life is rather capricious or meaningless, the most important thing is to enjoy the moment. In this environment, less thought is given to consequences, or even to death, since so little about it is known anyway. Existential experience has become a kind of end in itself. It also fits with the idea that since there is no metanarrative, there is little sense of accountability. People are their own judges of whether something is good or bad. All judgement has been reduced to one's personal preference.

One of the most important outcomes of this emphasis on personal experience is its impact on moral decision making. As mentioned earlier, morality involves a wide range of attitudes and actions, having to do (especially in this context) with how we relate to one another. The new morality, based on postmodern thought, is that one should never do anything that could potentially hurt someone else. The judge is not some outside authority such as government, one's employer, God, or biblical principle, but one's own sense of the matter. As previously stated, those kinds of conclusions are most often reached by way of a poll among friends.

One of the most emotionally intense issues of morality for people concerns sexual behaviour. As I said earlier, it is no secret that attitudes about sexual morality have changed radically in the last fifty years. In the former period, sexual mores were governed by an informed conscience based on criteria most often laid down by religion. But in these times, there is less interest in giving any attention to rationally constituted authority. Thus, decisions respecting sexual morality are considered a deeply personal matter. In these circumstances, society feels a new sense of liberty concerning appropriate sexual behaviour. The general conclusion is that the only standard of sexual engagement is mutual consent. By this standard, anything goes -- as long as the parties agree. It's all about satisfying one's own personal desires. In this environment, there is a bias against marriage, as it is considered an institutional relic of a former time. One should do what's expedient and practical rather than what may be expected from others, especially if they represent more traditional values.

The church, to say the least, has also been strongly impacted by these trends. Through the media, the arts, and politics, Christians are regularly challenged by the public about what it regards as outdated sexual ethics. The battle line is the church's understanding of God's decrees as grounded in the Bible, versus the new paradigm of postmodernism. The subject entails everything from appropriate sexual behaviour in general to extramarital sex and homosexuality. In the extreme, one of the most intense debates in certain parts of the church today concerns the reason for homosexual attraction and whether practicing homosexuals can marry as Christians and fully participate in the life of the church. But even among conservative evangelicals, it's not unusual to find more liberal attitudes towards premarital sex, common-law marriage, and a tendency to be less dogmatic about the immorality of homosexual attraction. As we shall see, these postmodern trends appear to also influence biblical interpretation.

The importance of one's own personal journey is at the heart of postmodern existentialism. As mentioned earlier, it was philosophers such as Kierkegaard and Kant who tried to legitimize the idea of personal experience as the essence of faith. Theologically, Karl Barth, the voluminous and influential theological writer of the last century (1886–1968), also contributed significantly to the importance of personal experience. Though he agreed with the idea of the Bible as objective revelation, he spoke of the completion of that revelation in terms of *illumination*. In other words, he elevated spiritual experience as a legitimate avenue of truly knowing God's Word. He spoke in terms of the Bible "becoming the Word of God," thus encouraging a kind of existential approach to a consideration of its authority.

There is much more that could be written about the significance of experience in postmodern culture, but one of the last things I will mention here is the degree to which this emphasis actually contributes to philosophical and moral relativism. Since personal experience has become the modus operandi of how people generally live their lives in a postmodern world, it's difficult to come to a consensus on questions of morality. In fact, this kind of impasse means that it's more likely for serious disagreement to develop among groups of people, at least on a deeper level. On the surface of things, they may appear to "live and let live," but when people begin to get hurt or killed because of serious differences, the spirit of the times can lead to anarchy and savagery. It's in that eventuality that we can see the great significance of various philosophical developments.

One other corollary of this emphasis on experience is the importance of friendships as a means of authenticating one's own experience. In other words, it doesn't work to self-actualize if the conclusion doesn't align with social relationship in some way. In that case, the world turns out to be a very lonely place. One needs to find at least a few people with whom he or she can share their experience. Since part of what it means to be alive in postmodern times involves engaging at least one other person in your experience, friendships are very important. These friendships needn't be very deep; one might, in fact, have many casual friendships. Nevertheless, friendships have the capacity to contribute greatly to existential experience.

In this chapter, I have enumerated some of the most distinctive characteristics of postmodernism. Following its intellectual roots, the cultural philosophy of these times disregards issues surrounding larger accountability towards God or others. An apt summary for the times might be the one we find in ancient Israel during the times of the judges: *"In those days there was no king in Israel. Everyone did what was right in his own eyes"* (Judges 21:25). In other words, in the absence of good leadership, people were left to their own devices. Today, largely because of suspicion and distrust, there exists a kind of disconnect between what is recognized as good authoritative leadership and people's own private interests. One way to interpret the current situation is as a deplorable lack of vision, and in the words of the ancient Jewish proverb, *"Where there is no vision, the people perish,"* (Proverbs 29:18, KJV). The English Standard Version says, *"the people cast off restraint."* I will have more to say concerning the matter of vision in the latter part of the book.

CHAPTER 6
Positive Outcomes of Postmodernism

In postmodernism, it's possible to conclude that Nietzsche's nihilism has come full circle. For those who are willing to give it deeper thought, it's obvious that there is much in the landscape of this cultural reality that appears very bleak. Having freed itself from the shackles of both pre-modernism and modernism (in which structures of authority tended to take precedence over emotional responses), postmodernism has emerged as a clear winner with its new emphasis on self-actualization. On one hand, it has left people everywhere with a deep sense of a spiritual and emotional void, as reflected in their busy lives, the multitude of their many pursuits and interests, and their constant sense of unsettledness. But on the other hand, the move towards postmodernism has opened up new and positive ways of thinking that provide fresh avenues of hope, especially from a Christian perspective. In other words, it's not all bad news. In fact, there are some very good outcomes of postmodernism that, if properly understood, can be utilized for good. As D. H. Lawrence is reputed to have said, "Ours is essentially a tragic age, so we refuse to take it tragically."

One way to think about the positive characteristics of today's generation is in terms of values. By values I simply mean those subconscious ideas about life that drive a person's deepest motivations. I'll have more to say about the importance of values in the section on postmodernism's relationship to Christian ministry, but the purpose of this section is to consider some of the positive values generally associated with postmodern culture.

One of the important things to remember about the change that has taken place is that the structuralism of modernism has been essentially dethroned. This factor is huge, for modernism certainly had its own sense of hubris, based on the pride of human intellect and accomplishment. Structures of authority built on human ingenuity and the scientific method ruled the cultural domain. Most arguments were constructed as logical and intellectual strong men. Even in the theological realm, those who could provide logically strong biblical arguments tended to win the day. Therefore, it was normal for a typical modern thinker to approach every challenge from a more rational perspective. In my own field of endeavour, sermons followed a logical sequence that consisted of a thesis and usually three alliterative points. Ministry methodology was highly structured with clear lines of direction and accountability.

It's true that the age of modernism represented a kind of rebellion against existing authority, but one of the reasons modernism hasn't survived is because its intellectually structured approach to life failed to address deeper notions of reality. The occurrence of two world wars near the end of the modern period also didn't help this approach. At the very least, those wars demonstrated that pure modern ways of thinking were not adequate to deal effectively with the most pressing social and political problems of our world. An argument might be made that it was intellectualism that contributed significantly to expressions of totalitarianism and the idea of world dominance. At the root of Stalin's deadly regime in Russia, for example, was a commitment to the intellectual philosophies of Karl Marx, Friedrich Engels, and Vladimir Lenin.

Therefore, in the natural evolution of philosophical thought, along with the breakdown of purely rational constructs, more attention also began to be given to the role of human emotion. While this attention to emotion alone can obviously lead to all kinds of difficulties, postmoderns have taught us that this element in the human psyche is not something to be ignored. Instead of treating emotion merely as an outcome of rational decisions (as moderns have done), postmoderns have tended to insist that emotion has its own kind of reason. Or as Blaise Pascal put it, "The heart has reasons which reason knows nothing about." Consistent with the postmodern idea that people can create their own reality, how we engage emotionally is a huge part of that reality. And that is the direction in which this section will lead. In fact, most of the values of postmodernism concern how we process matters on the level of our emotional experience.

Authenticity

Whereas modern thinking measured a person's credibility by their position of authority, however that was established, postmoderns more readily take someone seriously who demonstrates authenticity. This simply means that the person is real and genuine, that they are what you see, without façade. Moderns, it was thought, tended to hide behind formal credentials of one kind or another— age, seniority, education, reputation, conferred roles, position, life experience, and business or material success. But to the postmodernist, none of these qualities of assumed stature or station in life are considered important as ends in themselves. What matters is that people are themselves, that they are transparent, honest. It means that they have nothing to hide, as may have been true of a former generation. In the postmodern paradigm, people are commended for the fact that they are "real."

Thus, adults who wish to communicate effectively with their younger counterparts in any sphere must "tell it like it is." They need to be less guarded about the language they use, making themselves more vulnerable in the process. Just because a person has a certain educational degree, or has served in some notable institutional position, or has accomplished some important achievement, doesn't mean that they will have a significant impact on a listening audience. Effective communicators, both in formal and informal social encounters, are willing to speak candidly, especially if it means that they also talk about their failures.

Since communication has been an important aspect of my work as a pastor, I have noticed a significant change in the way pastors tend to communicate. Rather than focusing on the structured content of a biblical passage, for example, it seems that today's pastors tend to pick out one main theme from the text and develop that along the lines of story, often using illustrations from their own experience. Another tell-tale sign that today's pastor is trying to speak authentically is the tendency to preach extemporaneously instead of giving frequent attention to some detailed, prepared set of notes. This gives the impression that the person is simply being themselves, and to a postmodernist, nothing speaks louder than that kind of authenticity—even if the sermon tends to lack good expositional substance and application otherwise.

There are many illustrations of the authentic approach to social interactions. Another concerns the use of humour, or less formal language—even earthy or what some would consider foul language, like colloquialisms that refer to various bodily functions relating to elimination or sexual urge. (The reader can tell I write as a modern, because I'm not using the terms!) Some say that it is a way of "dumbing down" thoughts and ideas that were once considered too lofty to appreciate. There is often that kind of reaction to the modern tendency to be too formal.

In an earlier context, I wrote about styles of grooming and dress. Of course, there are lots of professions and occasions that still conform to more formal styles because of the perceived need to appear professional. Lawyers, representing one of the oldest institutions in the world, are inclined to dress formally. In general, where older institutions are taken seriously—weddings and funerals, high church gatherings, government business—people still dress rather officially. But increasingly formal dress has given way to "dumbed down" versions of the same, or formal dress itself is becoming a bit more casual. This tendency is all about seeking to be more authentic, more real, more one's true self, or true to oneself.

In all of this, there is a new interest, perhaps an actual appeal, in sharing the good as well as the bad about one's life. These days, people are more inclined to openly confess their shortcomings and failures, even if it is accompanied by some degree of shame or embarrassment. Such a confession will often include words to confirm one's genuineness, such as, "Well, at least I'm being honest." But it's important to note that such candidness isn't genuinely about serious shame. It's not likely that the person speaking of a lust or moral slip will think or speak of it as a sin. In that sense, there is a clear limit to the extent to which people are willing to share about their failures. Even in postmodernism, they aren't *that* vulnerable. Rather, the kind of transparency that I'm speaking about is simply a person's willingness to acknowledge that he or she is human and, in doing so, their willingness also to identify themselves with the rest of humanity. Such an admission is a human consciousness of failure, but not necessarily a God-consciousness of the same. But at least there is something refreshing about the fact that people today are less likely to be pretentious in contrast to the folks of the modern age.

It seems to me that this kind of authenticity can't help but be a positive thing. From a Christian perspective, it means that the more people are willing to be open about the doubts and misdeeds of their own lives, the more they may be willing to acknowledge their need for help. In some ways, compared to the modern period, people's willingness today toward authenticity represents a humbler attitude -- at least on the surface of things. This attitude has the potential to extend to more honest relationships, to deeper friendships, and to more effective ministry. On one hand, it is a refreshing change from the cold formality of a former period in which people were often led to hide behind their perceived success. On the other hand, too much transparency can lead to exploitation of others in one way or another, as in seeking to manipulate towards a positive response. And on another level, social honesty in this way might easily eclipse the need for true honesty with God and a true confession of sin in his sight. Ironically, it seems fair to say that in these postmodern times there appears to be less consciousness of sin or talk about it, even in the church.

Friendship and Community

I've already mentioned the significant role that friendships play in the postmodern world. This is due to several factors. One is that friendships provide some grounding amid an otherwise chaotic world. In the absence of a larger story that everyone embraces and that offers a reference point for the rest of life, relationships matter more than ever. People may not be able to relate to the past or the future with any degree of certainty, but they want to be fully alive in the present, making the most of every opportunity in an existential way. In the world of the existentialist, the greatest reality is one's immediate experience. More importantly, it is taking responsibility to create one's own reality by the exercise of one's will. Relationships with others offer a way to actualize one's identity, one's reality.

Furthermore, friendships offer the most immediate reference on how to deal with life's challenges. This is particularly true in matters of ethics and morality. Instead of looking to classic foundations on how to deal with moral issues, such as religion or various other rational authorities of the modern period, people are more likely to "look at the polls," or to ask their friends. Undoubtedly, that is why polling has become such a large industry in the Western world. Democracy, among postmodernists, has a new status, even higher than it had before. It is the new way of forming conclusions on important matters and in means of government. Even on ethical matters such as euthanasia, what wins the day is popular opinion. Therefore, the more people can be persuaded, by whatever means, to agree on a certain position, the more it is considered to be right.

This emphasis on friendship has received tremendous encouragement through recent advances in computer technology. Social media has been able to capitalize not only on our thirst for more information of every kind, but also on our evident great need for connection. By way of Facebook, Twitter, Instagram, Facetime, Linked-In, and a myriad of other social media devices, one can have many "friendships" with others who may or may not be particularly close to the one who initiates a comment. By these means, one can have connections with famous people, or people may become celebrated simply by these connections. Immediately and without delay, anyone can see or hear what their friends are doing and thinking, or influence a host of people to consider a certain perspective. The impact of social media as one of the outcomes of technical advance and postmodernism is nothing short of phenomenal.

Another reason why friendships have become so important is that despite today's capacity for immediate communication, there is an irony to all of it. Amid all social impulses and capacity for such, it seems that there is a heightened sense of loneliness. It's a little like the experience of the person who moves from the country to the big city hoping for more social advantages and opportunities, only to find that life in the big city is actually a very lonely existence. Ironically, because life in the city is busier and more complex, it is apparent that people have less value than they do in the small community. I have witnessed this first hand in my work as a transition pastor over the last ten years in a host of smaller communities where I have had the privilege of serving. There is a degree of connection and interdependence in the smaller community that often seems to be richer and stronger than what is evident in the larger center.

One reason for loneliness, which some would suggest has become epidemic in our modern world, is that there appear to be fewer good answers to life's big questions. In the absence of absolutes, people struggle with the reason for human existence. Depression and its affiliated mental illnesses are more common. Friendships offer some relief from the latent sense of despair that has become, just as Francis Schaeffer predicted, characteristic of our age. Friendships offer distraction from gloom; they offer love and mutual comfort. In this context, family connection is very important. Regardless of all the other deficiencies posited by postmodernism, it is one of the last and most important places to find something of the feeling and meaning of true love. But here too, there is somewhat of a contradiction because in postmodern times family relationships seem to have become more fragile. Perhaps, despite all the good intentions, married couples and families spend less time in actual communication with one another.

This reality, of the experience of loneliness and the search for friendship, is that people are looking for community, a place to belong. The quest for identity in self-actualization has a lot to do with belonging to a larger social entity. In that way, the search for community appears to be rather distinctive in these times. Whereas formerly the organizing principle for social community consisted of agreement with a belief system, today's search for community has more to do with the desire for recognition and love. In that sense, the reason for the group's existence is less important than it used to be. People want to be participants in groups because of the emotional need they feel to be loved and appreciated. What determines the value of a group is not so much its beliefs but the fact that one is accepted. This partially explains the recent phenomenon of young people leaving the comforts of Western culture to associate and enlist with terrorist organizations such as the Islamic State of Iraq and Syria (ISIS). In the grand scheme of things, the cause itself may be questionable, but the immediate satisfaction of belonging to a group that offers recognition and affirmation is more important.

This heightened interest in friendship and community, so characteristic of our times, should be viewed as a great opportunity for the Christian church. For one thing, the church offers the best opportunity for true love that the world has ever seen. Through the incarnation, life, death, and resurrection of Jesus Christ, the church's profession has been that God demonstrates the nature of true love -- spoken of as agape love in the classical Greek language.

More than anything else, it is this kind of self-sacrificing love that characterizes what the church is all about. Theologically, the church teaches that this kind of love depends on more than mere emotion, since it also involves the kind of action that goes beyond feeling. But many would argue that true, self-sacrificing, active love is primarily prompted by emotion—first from God towards us, then by our response to him, and finally in our love for one another.

The emotional need for love and acceptance in our times is, and can be, one of the most important motivations for engagement with the church today. It is in this context that we sometimes hear the adage "belonging before believing," meaning that a sense of belonging to the church comes before belief in its tenets. Whereas in former times confession of belief was a prerequisite for engagement in the church, the emphasis in this postmodern day is on making sure people feel loved and appreciated—even before they have any understanding of what Christian belief and the church is all about. It's all because emotional satisfaction has become such a large part of our lives in these times.

Obviously from a theological perspective, one can easily see the difficulty with this approach, as it might serve to minimize the importance of the acknowledgement of certain truths that ultimately, from a Christian perspective, provide the reason for faith. This illustrates one of the ongoing challenges of Christian ministry in today's world—the absence of interest in ultimate truth. But the reality of the deep emotional need that is so common today means that the church needs to work with this new paradigm in careful and constructive ways.

A good example of a ministry that has perceived this change and taken advantage of it is the ALPHA evangelism program developed by Reverend Nicky Gumbel of Holy Trinity Brompton, England. Typically, the event itself begins with a mealtime where people's friendships are developed. The meal is followed by a "video talk" in which Nicky Gumbel, often humorously, explains basic truths of the Christian faith. The talk is followed by an informally-led discussion with an emphasis on the invitation for everyone to ask any question they wish in relation to life or the Christian faith. The atmosphere is extremely light and emotionally appealing. On its website, Holy Trinity Brompton's primary appeal for participation is based on the idea of acceptance. As I write, a look at the website for the church, reveals this banner quote by Nicky Gumbel: *This is a church that loves and accepts everyone. You are welcome here.*[25]

There are many other ways for the church of today to "capitalize" on this great emotional longing for love and acceptance. One of the most popular ways to do this is through the church's initiative to organize small groups in which people may participate. Properly focused and led, small groups are a wonderful means of emphasizing acceptance without compromising on the essential biblical content of genuine faith. Another way for churches to make the most of this deeply-felt sense of need is through its pastoral care ministries, of which more will be written later.

The reality of today's world is that people feel emotionally lost. Without absolute truths to anchor their souls, they are feeling helpless on a very stormy ocean of individual opinion. The best answer for this huge emotional deficit is to know the love, recognition, acceptance, and affirmation that comes from God, as he has made himself known through the natural world, the Bible, his Son Jesus Christ, the gift of his Spirit, and the church.

---

25 Nicky Gumble, Holy Trinity Brompton, accessed January 3, 2016, https://www.htb.org/.

Justice and Compassion

Human suffering has always been a subject of great interest, simply because everyone, in one form or another, is the victim of suffering. Everyone in the world, sooner or later, is touched by natural disaster, relational conflict, serious loss of one kind or another, disease, and ultimately by death. Next to the reason for existence, human suffering is the greatest philosophical question of all time. For life to have any sense of meaning, human beings must be able to account for suffering and the very existence of evil.

In the pre-modern religious world of Christendom, suffering was always understood as the result of man's moral fall from grace through the temptation of the devil in the Garden of Eden (Genesis 3). Furthermore, in the Christian system of thought, the antidote for sin and suffering was provided by God through a comprehensive redemptive plan fulfilled in the coming of God's Son, Jesus Christ. In him, God made atonement for the sin of the world so that those who believe could experience forgiveness for sin, an effective way to deal with suffering, and the promise of eternal blessing in God's presence.

The modern period continued to capitalize on this message of the church, but it offered much more as well. Evangelicalism in its various forms emphasized the immediacy of divine power to overcome the effects of sin. After all, the Bible contains many examples of God's miraculous intervention for victory in battle, deliverance from disease, and provision of material blessing.

But with the coming of the modern age, with its emphasis on the acquisition of knowledge through rational inquiry, the church too expanded its resources for dealing more extensively with suffering. For one thing, it more readily accommodated and even encouraged scientific inquiry from a theological point of view, because it was perceived that scientific knowledge could aid in the relief of suffering. During the modern period, Christianity in its many forms took a great deal of interest in medical science. Later, this interest expanded to a Christian understanding of the social sciences such as psychology and sociology, and how their application could assist in dealing with human suffering. The modern period was a time of great educational expansion for the church, not only in the development of seminaries and Bible institutions, but also of universities specializing in how to relieve human suffering. In fact, it's well known that Christian educational institutions were the vanguard of educational expansion in the Western world.

At the same time, the church became more interested in matters of social justice, seeking to find ways to defend against political and economic oppression as it occurred around the world. For a large part of the Christian church, mission was not merely a matter of evangelism and church planting, but also very much about lifting people out of ignorance and material poverty. In Latin America, the Roman Catholic Church became known for the development of liberation theology—a theology that focused on overcoming political and economic oppression. At the same time and for similar reasons, but without the strong political agenda, the social gospel movement of the early nineteenth century gained considerable momentum, especially among the more theologically liberal Protestant churches of the West.

During seminary days in the early seventies, I and many of my seminary colleagues were impressed and influenced by the mission theorist Donald McGavran. He became known as the father of the modern church growth movement. That movement, which came about in some ways as a reaction to the social gospel concept, identified a principle it called *redemption and lift*. McGavran demonstrated that when a people group embraced the gospel of justification by faith, over time such a response positively impacted its economic and social status.

Considering the many biblical references to matters related to justice and compassion, it is not surprising that this should be a major theme in Christian ministry. But the concept of social justice has also come to enjoy a new and important status in these postmodern times. Once again, I believe this is largely due to the new interest and prominence of the role of human emotion. As the general population becomes increasingly sensitized, through visual media and other mediums, to the raw reality of human suffering, it can't help but feel the impact of that anguish on a deeply visceral level. Thus, works of charity have become a major new industry in Western culture, and not merely for the church. Compared to a few decades ago, today almost every business has some kind of annual charity drive. The notable increase in charitable giving is measurable through donations made for tax benefit purposes.[26] That measurement, however, doesn't consider the amount of philanthropy that takes place daily through the large number of informal personal community donations of money, food, and clothing.

Justice for the oppressed of every kind also appears to be a major theme of today's popular culture. We live in a highly sensitized and informed culture, familiar with instances of injustice towards minorities, the poor, and even the environment. Those who feel victimized by government, or even by business or neighbour, find it

---

26 "Charitable Giving Statistics," *National Philanthropic Trust*, accessed January 3, 2017 https://www.nptrust.org/philanthropic-resources/charitable-giving-statistics.

much easier to find a voice and the attention needed for their sense of justice. The legal business thrives, no doubt, on this reality.

In my work as a pastor, I have also seen this trend towards ministries of charity and justice on the increase in the church. In fact, the idea of mission in the church now has a whole new meaning than it did just a few decades ago. This follows upon the impetus that came from people like Frost and Hirsch, who in their book, *The Shaping of Things to Come*, wrote about transforming the Western church from an institutional, attractional model, to a more missional, apostolic one. "The whole tenor of this book," they write, "will be to call post-Christendom to see itself again as *missionary movement* rather than as an institution."[27]

By "missionary movement," these writers are not talking about methods of evangelism and church-planting peculiar to the modern period, but about the focus of the missional church movement of these postmodern times being "getting dirty for Jesus." It's about embodying the nature of the gospel as an expression of God's love for the sake of ministry to the poor and downtrodden. It's about being willing to leave the church building to get involved in the community as "the hands and feet of Jesus," and to become involved in community concerns with a view to changing them to reflect more of Jesus' kingdom principles.

Considered from a critical perspective, it's perceived that the church is not so much about proclamation and conversion as it is about demonstrating the love of Jesus through deeds of kindness and compassion. I have known of churches in my own denomination that, at least once a year, cancel their Sunday morning service in order to do a variety of charitable works in the community during

---

27 Frost and Hirsch, 16.

that time. By doing so, these church leaders hope to demonstrate, both to their parishioners and the community, that the church is much more than a cloistered religious community—that it truly is about going out from the church to do God's kingdom work.

There is much more to be said about social justice and compassion as a very positive change in many respects. Postmoderns would say that we should stop trying to figure out the meaning of life in terms of origin and destiny. Instead, we should think existentially about human existence, focusing on relationships with people and real human need. After all, remember, "people don't really care how much you know until they know how much you care." Rather than spending our time trying to convince people of the merits or truth of Christianity, postmoderns say, we need to simply love them in their place and time of need. First and foremost, Christians should be known for their deeds of love and service in Christ's name; theological truth, in this context and culture, evidently, is of secondary importance.

Passion

Last night at the grocery store, the young girl at the check-out counter asked me a typical postmodern question, one which I have also heard often from servers in restaurants: "Do you have plans for the rest of your evening?" At first glance, it sounds like a rather benign question of human interest. In the modern period, a stranger would never think to ask this kind of personal question, especially of one who is obviously considerably older than the person asking. Yet today, this kind of personal interchange is not uncommon. It reflects a significant departure from the cold, sterile formality of the modern period. The question is postmodern because it is personal, informal (without sensitivity to age or station in life), and comes with a certain outward sense of emotional interest. One can't help but agree that such an expression of personal interest is an attractive change.

In postmodern times, feelings are not to be taken lightly. One of the indications of this change is the frequent reference to the concept of passion. In the words of the old cliché, "if I had a dollar every time I heard the word passion these days, I'd be a very rich man indeed!" Passion speaks of intense emotion. It has to do with the exclamation of deep feelings of romantic love, but also of powerful conviction concerning some important cause.

It can be said that passion, in the context of postmodernism, is the new "rationale." It is definitely equal, or even more important, than cognitive processes of logic. This fits well with the very nature of postmodernism as a reaction to the pure rationalism of a former time. Passion is considered an appropriate expression of self-actualization and the creation of one's own reality. To the extent that emotion defines the movement, passion is at the heart of postmodernism.

It should be noted, especially of interest from a Christian perspective, that there is an undisciplined element to postmodern passion. Sometimes this is spoken of as Dionysian passion in recognition of the Greek god, Dionysus. In Greek mythology, Dionysus represented ecstatic, orgiastic expression. The dictionary defines Dionysus as:

> ... a Greek god, son of Zeus and Semele, also
> called Bacchus. Originally a god of fertility,
> associated with wild and ecstatic religious rites, in
> later traditions he is a god of wine who loosens

inhibitions and inspires creativity in music and poetry.[28]

Probably it's not incidental that the consumption of wine in the West has increased exponentially in the last fifty years or so. One US statistic reports that the annual consumption of 53 million gallons of wine in 1960 has grown to 779 million in 2015.[29] According to an article in the *Toronto Star*, written by Lisa Wright in 2015, Canada's consumption of wine now ranks seventh in the world.[30] If wine consumption is a sign of prosperity, it is also very much an indication of a change in focus towards the experience of passion. It may also reflect something of the change of attitude about wine consumption among more conservative Christians. Evidently, a former restriction based on biblical references to abstinence (i.e. Proverbs 20:1; 23:29-35) has given way in these postmodern times to other biblical references that encourage an expression of celebration with wine (i.e. Proverbs 3:9–10; John 2:1-11).

More commonly in today's Western culture, passion refers to the interest people have in relationships, movies, music, sport, and even food. Movies are geared, more than anything it seems, to incite intense passion about love and hate. Even the daily news tries to reflect a strong sense of emotion. It's been said that if something

28   *The Canadian Oxford Dictionary*, "Dionysius," Katherine Barber, Gen. ed. (Don Mills, ON: Oxford University Press, 1998), 394.

29   "Wine Consumption in the U.S.," *Wine Institute*, accessed on January 3, 2017, https://www.wineinstitute.org/resources/statistics/article86.

30   Lisa Wright, "Canada Among the Top Producers of Imported Wine," *Business, The Toronto Star*, February 17, 2015, accessed January 3, 2017, https://www.thestar.com/business/2015/02/17/canada-among-the-worlds-top-consumers-of-imported-wine.html.

is worth doing at all, it's worth doing with great enthusiasm and passion. In a new way, it is passion that gives life meaning—an extension of the existentialist experience. How often these days do we hear the Latin words, "Carpe Diem," meaning, "Seize the day!"

It is interesting to me to see how this obsession with passion is also evident in both the content and method of Christian ministry. Some of the most popular Christian ministry leaders reflect a deep sense of passion in their personalities and preaching. This might well be the most identifying feature of contemporary Christian leaders such as Louie Giglio (pastor of Passion City Church), Francis Chan (pastor and author of books like *Crazy Love*), or Andy Stanley (pastor of North Point Ministries, Atlanta). These are Christian leaders of influence today who are often admired and applauded for their passion as much as the content of their message.

Often equally important is their call to passionate Christian faith and commitment. In this latter sense, passion is considered a legitimate expression of the very nature of what it means to be a disciple of Jesus Christ. Biblically, there is no room for half-hearted commitment in being a true follower of Christ. So, there is, among postmodern Christians, a call to radical commitment, something often defined in terms of a very active, culturally-engaged kind of faith. For this reason, Christian postmodernists love to preach and teach from the Gospels, or those portions of scripture like James, that challenge "believers" to action. In fact, being "a disciple of Jesus," rather than simply "a believer" (based on a verbal confession of faith in Jesus Christ) has become the favoured way of referring to a true Christian.

Another rather beautiful expression of passion in the context of Christian ministry involves the matter of worship. I have mentioned earlier how Christian worship has moved from the more formal, theologically rich hymnody of the modern period to a more intense, passionate chorus-singing of these postmodern times. One caricature of this change might be to speak of it as a move from the cathedral-like sounds of the church organ to the intense rhythmic sounds of a rock band drum (while also accompanied by many other kinds of percussion, wind, and string instruments). Reflective of the greater interest in passion, worship in today's typical church could easily include physical movement such as hand-waving, banner-waving, and even dance. It also will likely involve some form of free-verse in the lyrics, more electrically-amplified volume, and a strong element of repetition. It seems rather obvious that a large part of Christian worship today is really all about passion.

Many would agree that these examples of expressions of passion, as well as the call to radical fervent commitment, are a good thing. Postmodern thinking has served effectively to engage Christians in a greater sense of spontaneous worship, in generous acts of charity on many levels, and in radical mission activities. There is much in the Bible that commends this deep sense of emotional response to God and his revelation. In their focus on biblical analysis, Christians of a former generation have often sadly missed this emotional expression of faith. It helps us understand better what David voiced in Psalm 40:6–8, when he said:

> In sacrifice and offering you have not delighted,
> but you have given me an open ear. Burnt offer-
> ing and sin offering you have not required. Then
> I said, "Behold, I have come; in the scroll of the
> book it is written of me: I delight to do your will,
> O my God; your law is within my heart."[31]

---

31 Unless otherwise indicated, biblical references are from the English Standard Version, Wheaton, IL: Crossway, 2001.

> As a deer pants for flowing stream, so pants my
> soul for you, O God. My soul thirsts for God, for
> the living God. When shall I come and appear
> before God? (Psalm 42:1–2).

It must also be acknowledged that there is a negative, almost sinister, side to this great interest in passion. On the one hand, if one isn't careful, there may easily be in it a new motivation to indulge the more carnal aspects of human desire for its own sake. Moderns especially would be inclined to warn against the idea of feelings or passions themselves being the reason for anything. Moderns have always tended to stand against that old notion, "If it feels good, do it!" At the same time, since it is obvious that the Creator intended for human beings to experience physical and emotional pleasure, moderns have probably often been too quick to judge something as morally wrong simply for that reason.

One other danger of the pursuit of passion is that its obsession, in major matters and in small, can easily lead to misguided conclusions about what's right or wrong. Passion itself is ultimately no substitute for substance. The problem with passion is that it is often inclined to ignore deeper questions of reality that can only be appreciated through rational inquiry. In Christian ministry, for example, the tendency these days is to avoid topics like the judgement of hell, partly because of the negative emotions the subject elicits. It is imperative, especially in line with Christian thought, that all passion be guided or checked by what we think of as the more objective truth of scripture. The difficulty here is obvious. One of the great challenges of life in these postmodern times is in how we seek to determine what is objectively true, both in life or even in the Bible. The latter concerns that important matter called biblical hermeneutics, which I will address in the next chapter.

Organic Spirituality

One of the outcomes of the Age of Reason and modernism was the parallel development of the Industrial Revolution. The modern period was certainly a time of empirical development in more ways than one. It was a time of imperial expansion and colonization, not only for commercial purposes, but also for the sake of the extension of the church and its mission. Much of it, of course, had to do with the acquisition of wealth as the ultimate measure of success and personal wellbeing. The mass production of goods, including agricultural products, was enhanced by the importance of scientific developments of the time.

But it is also to this pride of rationalism and these practical developments to which postmoderns have reacted so strenuously. Having seen much of the ill effects of modernism in these ways, they have yearned for a greater sensitivity towards indigenous values. This is also consistent with ideas especially relevant to postmodernism, such as existential personal experience, and the development of small homegrown communities.

I have a young friend who has spent several years working professionally among aboriginal people on British Columbia's west coast. As a typical postmodernist, he does not subscribe to any metanarrative that attempts to explain the reason for human existence in terms of absolute truth. Though he recognizes many benefits in the history of Christianity and the church, he also feels that this kind of religious thinking has had many negative effects. It is interesting to note that he once referred to himself as a "social anarchist," by which he meant that he is opposed to large bureaucratic systems of government that seek to control and subjugate peoples for their own benefit. Social anarchism is a way of affirming the kind of individual freedom that postmoderns emphasize, while at the same time recognizing the need for some kind of mutual dependence in community—something about which I wrote earlier.

"Organic" is a popular reference in current culture to anything that concerns natural development as opposed to scientifically modified intervention for the sake of mass production. Essentially, the term refers to that which derives from living matter, but in today's use it has become synonymous with wholesomeness and health. Most often, we think of it in an agricultural context in which products are grown without the assistance of chemical fertilizers, pesticides, and genetically modified organisms (GMOs), which potentially could be the cause of various kinds of human illnesses and disease.

"Organic" also refers to natural origins, wholeness, and completeness, and of being at one with nature. It belongs largely to the language of ecological balance and environmental appreciation. Its huge, all-encompassing approach to life makes it a kind of subset of postmodern philosophy and culture.

This organic idea has not only affected the way people today approach their dietary preferences, but also how they approach many other aspects of daily life, including an obsession with physical fitness, recreational activity (with a new special interest in camping and exploring the wilderness), and concern for the protection of the environment (through huge efforts at recycling and sustainable development). Pure postmoderns believe that human beings should not think of themselves as superior to other forms of life—especially animals, but also plant life. I've heard it said, for example, in criticism of Christianity that this idea of human superiority over the animals is rooted in the Genesis account of creation that provided for humankind's dominion over the animals and natural world.

One effect of this organic approach to life is pantheism, which professes that God and nature are actually the same, or that God is at one with nature. In other words, people should expect to encounter God in the spirit of animals and trees. This idea is not unique to postmodern times, but it clearly demonstrates, in its rejection of the Christian metanarrative, where postmodern thinking may ultimately lead. In Romans 1, Saint Paul expresses what Christians believe to be God's decree about this sort of thinking:

> Claiming to be wise, they became fools, and exchanged the glory of the immortal God for images resembling mortal man and birds and animals and creeping things. Therefore, God gave them up in the lusts of their hearts to impurity, to the dishonoring of their bodies among themselves, because they exchanged the truth about God for a lie and worshiped the creature rather than the Creator, who is blessed forever! Amen (Romans 1:22–26).

Notwithstanding the possible difficulties with extreme organic-like thinking, there is much in it that is commendable from a philosophical and theological point of view. One of the positive outcomes is the new sense of respect that has been conferred on God's created order of things. It's right that humanity should regard the whole of the natural world as a beautiful gift that needs to be guarded from various kinds of abuse. From a Christian perspective, we should learn to live with God's creation in utilitarian ways, being careful at the same time that the world or cosmos doesn't become its own object of worship. Despite the possible distortions of reality, postmodernism has contributed significantly to help us appreciate more deeply the wonder and beauty of the natural world. Properly regarded, as the Bible also affirms in Romans 1:19–20, the natural world has much to tell us about the very nature of God himself. Our job is to ensure the measured use of the earth's resources instead of its careless abuse.

"Organic" also has many positive allusions to how Christians live their daily lives, as well as their experience of vibrant spirituality. The emphasis on wholesome diet and recreation is not only a good thing for our personal health, but also for the development of any local community, because it fosters interdependence. Properly understood, organic thinking flies in the face of an "us and them" kind of dualism. It's also good for Christians to understand that we must communicate with one another honourably and deal more constructively together with the challenges of living in our wonderful world.

Due to the influence of postmodern thinking, the way in which Christians think of spirituality and Christian ministry has changed significantly. For one thing, Christians are often inclined to want to study the Bible more inductively, by which I mean that they are trying to read and apply it at face value, just as if they were reading it for the first time. This is an organic approach to Bible study as opposed to a more deductive approach in which the reading of the Bible proceeds with preconceived theological ideas. In organic Bible study, a person is asking the question of what the text actually says, what it means today (the hermeneutical question), and how it might be applied to a person's life. An important caution in this approach is that the student of the Bible must guard against the development of conclusions that do not necessarily represent "the whole counsel of God," a benefit of systematic theology. But the refreshment of this approach is that the reader is seeking a more immediate (emotional) connection with the divine Author through listening to God's Spirit in this process.

Organic spirituality has also been a factor in Christians pursuing greater intimacy with God through the exercise of various kinds of spiritual disciplines. Daily Bible reading and prayer potentially take on new meaning in this context, because these are now viewed as part of a much larger series of disciplines that can greatly aid in cultivating a growing relationship with God. Though once the greater domain of Roman Catholic theology as a means of contemplation, it has been shown that spiritual disciplines of all kinds were also a large part of early church life and ministry. Many have written about the significance of various spiritual disciplines as a practical means to experiencing practical holiness.

One of the earlier influences among evangelical Christians towards the practice of the spiritual disciplines was Richard Foster. In his book, *Celebration of Discipline,* he writes about the disciplines of meditation, prayer, fasting, study, simplicity, submission, service, solitude, confession, and worship:

> God has given us the Disciplines of the spiritual life as a means of receiving his grace. The Disciplines allow us to place ourselves before God so that he can transform us.[32]

Many others have written about the importance of the spiritual disciplines, some of my favourite being Dallas Willard, Marjorie Thompson, Bruce Demarest, and a Roman Catholic writer, Henri Nouwen. A more recent example of the significance of the spiritual disciplines from my own tradition is one called *God in My Everything,* by Ken Shigematsu. *Forming the Leader's Soul,* by Morris Dirks, deals with the related ministry of pastoral spiritual

---

32 Richard Foster, *Celebration of Discipline* (San Francisco: Harper Collins, 1978), 7.

direction. I may not agree with everything these authors postulate on this subject, but there is undoubtedly an interest in the spiritual disciplines in these times as an extension of the idea of organic spirituality.

This practice of the spiritual disciplines is based on the biblical concept of "being conformed to the image of God's Son," as expressed in Romans 8:29. This is understood as a process toward maturity in practical holiness. Other biblical references that strengthen this idea include 2 Corinthians 3:18, which speaks of *"beholding the glory of the Lord … being transformed into the same image from one degree of glory to another,"* and Galatians 4:19, where Saint Paul speaks of, *"being in the anguish of childbirth until Christ is formed in you."* All of these references emphasize that true holiness is more than initial faith in Christ (or even of a critical sanctification experience of one kind or another) at some point in time. Rather, the exercise of the spiritual disciplines involves the whole of one's Christian life experience. It is a more holistic view of the nature of the Christian faith, something that speaks of its organic nature in contrast simply, to a faith that merely consists of a series of doctrinal beliefs. Once again, it is evident that this organic approach to the Christian faith is directed towards a deeper emotional, relational experience with God.

It wasn't that long ago that the emphasis in discipling new Christians, and even in evangelism, was on helping people intellectually grasp and personally respond to a system of beliefs. Evangelism employed the type of presentation that affirmed four basic truths: the existence and nature of God (John 3:16), the fact that everyone is born with a sinful nature and thus estranged from God, incurring his eternal judgement (Romans 3:23 and 6:23), that God's provision for man's sin problem was Jesus' incarnation, atoning sacrifice, and bodily resurrection (Romans 5:8), and that a personal confession through a simple prayer of faith in Christ was necessary for assurance of eternal salvation (Romans 10:9, 10; 1 John 5:13). A small tract called *The Four Spiritual Laws*, prepared by Bill Bright, founder of Campus Crusade for Christ, was iconic as a method of this kind of evangelism. Through its use in many different contexts and languages throughout the world, tens of thousands of people began their Christian spiritual journey. There are many other examples of this kind of evangelistic approach, including *The Roman Road*, *Evangelism Explosion*, and *The Way of the Master*.

Today's generation tends to shy away from the use of this kind of structured approach in evangelism, often expressing the critique that it is too simplistic in its explanation and outcomes. It seriously questions whether a simple prayer can really be the means of becoming a Christian. Consistent with the idea of a more organic approach to introducing the Christian faith, today's "evangelist" would emphasize the discipleship paradigm of what it means to become a Christian. In fact, almost entirely to the exclusion of references to "evangelism," "discipling" has become the new means of describing the introduction of others to faith in Jesus Christ. This change reflects one of the ways in which the church has come to view the nature of faith and evangelistic ministry. I'll attempt to explain more of this change in the next chapter, which will also outline some of the challenges that postmodernism presents to the Christian faith.

The interest in organic spirituality also extends to a couple of other noticeable expressions of faith among postmodern millennials. At first sight, the two seem somewhat contradictory, but that fact only serves to demonstrate the apparent extremes in postmodernism. One is a return for some evangelicals to more liturgical forms of worship. Church liturgy is attractive to postmoderns because, like the appeal of the spiritual disciplines which are rooted in early and medieval Christianity, many millennials have a special regard for church tradition. Perhaps it provides for a sense of awe and reverence in the midst of the prevailing sense of chaos that exists otherwise. Also, consistent with the interest in organic spirituality and the importance of existential experience, liturgy offers a mystical dimension to worship. On the other hand, many millennials also appear to want to distance themselves from a mere confessional form of the Christian faith in favour of a more radical action kind of faith. They might be inclined to say that Christianity is not so much about what happens in the church as what happens outside the church. They prefer active expressions of faith in the world in contrast to worship in an institutional context. This interest in active Christian discipleship by this means also reflects a desire for organic spirituality.

It's important to recognize that some of the movement from modernism to postmodernism is of great blessing and benefit to how we speak about and practice Christian faith and ministry. While modernism has much to commend it regarding the importance of a reasoned, cognitive approach to life, postmodernism has been successful in teaching us that reason alone is insufficient for understanding and experiencing life and the Christian faith. Though postmodernism may have many difficulties and shortcomings, one of its great blessings to the world, and even the church, is that it has taught us in a new way about the tremendous importance of the emotional dimension of our lives.

CHAPTER 7

Christian Faith Challenges in Postmodern Times

For anyone interested in finding out about basic Christianity, the Gospels are the first stop, because they are considered the most organic expression of what early Christianity was all about. That's because Matthew, Mark, Luke, and John focus on the life and ministry of Jesus. The first three are called "the Synoptics," because they give very parallel views, by three different writers, of many of the same events surrounding Jesus' activities and teachings. The genuineness of these texts is partly established through the variations in what is often spoken of as "eyewitness accounts" concerning Jesus. Their differences are partly due to the fact that the three wrote for different audiences—Matthew for the Jews, Mark (who evidently took much of his material from Peter) for more of a Roman audience, and Luke, who later became a companion of Paul's and was a medical doctor, for Greek readers. John's gospel, written quite a bit later than the others, is also an account of Jesus' life and ministry. It appears to have more theological intention, partly to counter false ideas in Greek thought concerning the identity of Christ.

By means of these gospels, we are able to acquire a pretty comprehensive and accurate understanding of what Jesus' life and work was all about. The Gospels give us a glimpse of the birth and early life of Jesus, but focus attention mainly on his introduction by John the Baptist, and then his ministry to the people of Judea and Galilee. Much of what we read in the Gospels attends to Jesus' introduction of the Kingdom of God, his miraculous ministries of compassion to people who trusted him for his help, his teachings, and his special work of calling and training his disciples. There is also a good deal of material on how he interacted with those who challenged his identity and teaching. All the Gospels speak extensively about his arrest by Jewish authorities, his unjust trial before them and the Roman rulers of the time, his excruciating suffering and death on a rough wooden cross, and his glorious resurrection.

The special point of interest for our purposes in this chapter is how it is evident in the Gospels that while Jesus' life and ministry was positively received by a good number of people, including his disciples, it was also vehemently opposed by others who eventually were responsible for his death. At the worst point of his suffering, just prior to his death, even his own disciples didn't have the fortitude of faith to stand with him. And, so it is that we might well ask why a man who displayed such unusual kindness and care (doing much of it miraculously), and who spoke such wonderful words of wisdom and authority, should end up with so much animosity, eventually leading to his terrible crucifixion.

It's important to recognize that the Christian perspective of Jesus, based on the New Testament records, has always been that his life and ministry were unique and distinctive in a variety of ways, factors which also made him a special target of opposition. For one thing, there was the matter of his miraculous powers displayed in ways that challenged people's best understanding of the laws of nature. These included such notables as turning water into wine (John 2:1–11), the unusual catch of fish (Luke 5:1–11), his calming of the storm (Matthew 8:23–27), his miraculous feeding of the five thousand (recorded by all four gospels, including Mark 6:30–44), his walking on water (Mark 6:45–52), his incredible feeding of the four thousand (Matthew 15:32–39), the finding of the temple tax in a fish's mouth (Matthew 17:24–27), the rapid withering of the fig tree (Mark 11:12–14), and a second miraculous catch of fish (John 21:4–11).

Jesus also performed many miraculous healings from disease, such as the healing of Peter's mother-in-law (Luke 4:38–39), the miraculous recovery of the Roman centurion's servant (Matthew 8:5–13), his unusual curing of two blind men (Matthew 9:27–31), his remedial work of a man who was deaf and dumb (Mark 7:31–37), and his healing touch of the high priest's servant's ear during his own arrest in the Garden of Gethsemane (Luke 22:50–51). Many of these are mentioned by more than one of the Gospels.

There were also cases of liberation from evil spirits, as in the case of the man who was freed from an evil spirit by Jesus' command in the synagogue in Capernaum (Luke 4:31–36). Another notable case involved one or two men who were possessed by many demons, across the lake of Galilee in the country of the Gadarenes. When Jesus commanded the demons to leave, they went into a herd of pigs that rushed into the lake and drowned (see Matthew 8:28–34 or Luke 8:26–39). Another case involved the release from an evil spirit of the daughter of a Gentile woman who begged him for mercy for her daughter -- which evidently happened without his actual presence with the girl (Mark 7:24–30). These unusual stories seemed to be a regular part of Jesus' ministry. In Matthew 4:23 we read, *"And he went throughout all Galilee, teaching in their synagogues and proclaiming the gospel of the kingdom and healing every disease and every affliction among the people."*

Perhaps even more compelling are stories of Jesus raising people from the dead, such as the case of the daughter of Jairus, the synagogue leader in Mark 5:21–43, or of the widow's son in Luke 7:11–16, or of Lazarus after he had been dead for several days in John 11. The greatest case of all, to which all the gospel writers attest, was Jesus' own resurrection only three days after his death by crucifixion (see Matthew 28:1–15).

These miracles point powerfully to Jesus' uniqueness as a person—not only because of how they challenged the existing laws of nature and effects of suffering, but also because of their expression of compassion for people in great need. These stories contributed greatly to his fame as a healer and worker of miracles at that time, but also to his reputation as a man of great care and compassion.

Yet sometimes his very deeds also caused consternation and disagreement. This was especially so when he challenged existing superficial notions of true spirituality. Examples of this include the case of Jesus and his disciples ignoring the ceremonial cleansing of his hands before they ate (Mark 7:1–23), his healing of a man's hand on the Sabbath (Mark 3:1–6), and he and his disciples picking grain ("harvesting") on the Sabbath (Matthew 12:1–8).

His miracles of healing, deliverance from demons, and resurrections were not the only reason for his uniqueness, popularity, and opposition. His distinctiveness was also due to the words that he spoke. A large collection of his teachings is found in what has come to be called The Sermon on the Mount, found in Matthew 5, 6, and 7. The essence of his message in that sermon is about the deeper meaning of the Old Testament Law in terms of attitude of heart as opposed to mere outward acts. Without relaxing any of these deeper requirements of the Law, he spoke of his own purpose to fulfil it (Matthew 5:17). Later, he spoke of how the entire Old Testament Law could be summed up in two commands: "to love the Lord your God with all your heart, soul, and mind; and to

love your neighbour as yourself" (Matthew 22:37–40). Again and
again, after Jesus spoke to the crowds who gathered to see and
hear him, the Gospels record that they were "astonished" by his
teachings and the authority with which he spoke (Matthew 7:28–29;
Luke 4:22; 4:32).

The most astounding confession of Jesus himself, as well as
of his disciples, was that he was the Son of God. This was the
essence of the discussion that took place between Jesus and his
disciples at Caesarea Philippi as recorded in Matthew 16:13–20. It
was also the main thrust of John's gospel. He came to this world
as the divine Logos, the very essence of God in a human body
(John 1:1–3), and there is no doubt that, despite his unusual appeal
otherwise, this became the reason for his greatest offense, which I
describe subsequently.

Despite all that Jesus said so truthfully and beautifully, it
quickly became evident that not everyone appreciated the words
that he spoke, because sometimes his words pointed very directly
to the unbelief and resistance in the hearts and minds of the people.
Very early in his time of service, some of the people in his hometown synagogue in Nazareth tried to push him over a cliff, because
they didn't believe him when he said he had come as the fulfilment
of Isaiah's prophecy (Luke 4; Isaiah 61). Repeatedly, Jesus had to
contend with a spirit of doubt concerning his origin, identity, and
power. Sometimes this even happened among the twelve he had
chosen as his disciples. They often struggled with such things as
fear in the midst of the storm (Matthew 14:22–31), doubts about
his ability to provide, questions about what he meant (Matthew
16:5–12), or even his identity (Matthew 16:13–20). Within the
larger crowd of his disciples, there were those who were troubled
by the words that he spoke and the challenges he presented
(John 6:60–71).

But by far, Jesus' strongest disapproval came from the religious leaders of his day, especially the Pharisees and members of the Sanhedrin, the center of Jewish power and authority. Often the Pharisees would listen on the side-lines to see if they could trap him with their questions, but they were always stymied by his response. Once they asked him his opinion on divorce (Matthew 19:3–9), which evidently was a common practice among them. His answer was to turn them back to the spirit of the Law regarding marriage, which they had obviously disregarded. In another case, they tried to test his loyalty to Caesar by asking whether it was right to pay taxes to him (Matthew 22:15–22). Again, his answer left them speechless. At various times, they tried to arrest him. On one occasion, they sent their policemen to capture him, but when they came back and were asked why they didn't bring him in, they answered, *"No one ever spoke like this man!"* (John 7:46). In the end, when his time had *"fully come"* (John 7:8), through the betrayal of one of his own disciples, they arrested Jesus and executed a mock trial that quite quickly led to his execution by crucifixion.

Even though Jesus was perfectly virtuous in all his deeds and words, it's important to note that he faced disagreement on many fronts, due in part to his unusual personal reputation, of which many were jealous. They also opposed the fact that he identified himself as the Son of God because of the exclusiveness this implied in terms of religious and philosophical thought. For example, John quotes him as saying, *"I am the way, and the truth, and the life. No one comes to the Father except through me,"* (John 14:6). In Acts 4:12, Peter preached in Jerusalem, *"... there is salvation in no one else, for there is no other name under heaven given among men by which we must be saved."*

Jesus' claim to deity and the exclusive means of salvation has always been foundational to Christian theology, and it is this concept, perhaps more than any other, that brings Christianity into such sharp conflict with postmodernism. This kind of exclusivity isn't limited to Christian theology, as exclusiveness is often the very nature of religious ideology. It would be dishonest to say that Christianity is alone in its sense of exclusivity. In fact, it could be argued that postmodernism itself is a religious ideology with certain intolerant views and convictions concerning the nature of reality. For example, at its core, postmodernism asserts the human self as the prime reference for any judgement concerning reality. By doing so, it confesses to a kind of religious perspective. It also accepts the idea of religious pluralism, which asserts that every religion is basically the same by virtue of the moral standard of love and care for neighbour that all religions promote.

Christianity has no quarrel with postmoderns or any other religious system concerning our moral responsibility of love and care for neighbour, but it disagrees about the essence of moral responsibility, in terms of true righteousness, and in how it may be achieved. It comes down to the relative difference between opinions on the nature of truth. Postmoderns insist that there is no such thing as absolute truth, no metanarrative that completely and universally explains reality. Accordingly, they would say, we can only speak in terms of "my truth," or "truth for me." This means that no one is in any position to judge another's ideas or behaviour, if such behaviour isn't hurtful to someone else.

Christianity, on the other hand, is fundamentally committed to the idea that truth exists, in an objective sense, as something separate from human experience. This idea is based on the view that God is a personal God who exists apart from the world he has made (that he is transcendent). In fact, Christians would say that this conception of God is universally innate in human understanding and experience because of what is seen in the natural world (Romans

1:20). But they would also go on to say that our understanding of this transcendent God is clarified by the distinct revelation that has come to us from God in the Holy Scriptures, and in what they say to us concerning the person and ministry of Jesus Christ. The standard of moral righteousness he represents is absolutely pure, something that he requires from his moral creatures, and only achievable through faith in Christ (Ephesians 2:8, 9).

Furthermore, Christians believe that the Bible as we have it today, despite some very small instances of textual translation difference, is a completely reliable document of God's words through the prophets and apostles, not only for his own people, but for the entire world. In other words, based on a long history of honest scholarship, diligent historical and archaeological research, as well as vigorous attention to matters of language and culture, Christians insist that the Bible is a pure revelation of God's will when compared to any other religious idea or document. Much more has been written on the uniqueness of the Christian view, but this is the essence of the reason for the strong difference between Christianity and postmodernism.

The purpose of this book, in part, is to acknowledge the seriousness of this difference, its impact on the development of Western culture, and its implications for the life and ministry of the church. In the first place, it is important to recognize that conflict in our world has always existed from the time of Adam's disobedience in the Garden of Eden. Biblical literature is rife with the reality of conflict between God and Satan, between good and evil, between righteousness and wickedness, and between God's people and the world. Though the very mention of such a conflict will tend to be offensive to today's postmoderns, the fact is that conflict is a major theme in the history of the Jewish people, as well as the Christian church. Christian theologians maintain that the reality of conflict itself is one of the great consequences of the curse brought into existence by the disobedience of Adam and Eve, our first parents, in the Garden of Eden (Genesis 3). "The Fall," as it has been called, resulted in a state of disharmony in relationship to God, one another, within nature itself, and in the relationship between humanity and the natural order.

One of the reasons for disharmony between people is because of the way they relate to God. This is well illustrated by the conflict and terrible consequence in the relational breakdown between the world's first siblings, Cain and Abel (Genesis 4). It seemed to have arisen over Cain's offense at God's acceptance of Abel's sacrifice instead of his own. In other words, the very first serious conflict, which resulted in Abel's death by the hands of his brother Cain, was due to a religious exercise in which one person seemed to connect with God while the other did not. It would be wrong to ignore that this is the reason for a good deal of conflict throughout human history. It illustrates that religious differences between people can be significant, based on their perception or reality of divine blessing.

One of the realities of the emergence of postmodernism is the ideological conflict that has ensued, especially with Christianity. This kind of conflict is not something new for Christianity, just as ideological conflict was not something new for the Jews of Old Testament times. Historically, there is no question that there have been times when Jews and Christians have been on the wrong side of conflict. There are many instances in which both, as part of God's own judgement towards them, have been victims of their own ignorance and arrogance. Nevertheless, there are many other examples of times when Jews and Christians were treated unjustly and violently persecuted because of their ideological views, and it could easily be said that this is one of the possible outcomes for the church in today's postmodern world. Jesus said, "*If they persecuted me, they will persecute you also… They will treat you this way because of my name, for they do not know the One who sent me*" (John 15:20, 21 NIV).

At various times, it appears that there is a new wave of anti-Christian sentiment in the world, and it appears, at times, that this can be very strong. Christianity has often come to be regarded as more of an enemy than an ally of that which is good and right. Today, Christianity is sometimes seen as the cause of many of the problems that exist in the world. It is often blamed, for example, for being at the heart of colonial expansion, which often took advantage of vulnerable peoples. Though Christians may protest that there were many other factors at play in colonial expansion, or that there were many instances of genuine beneficence that came by way of the church in these times, it is often taken for granted that Christianity was at the root of all the difficulties that arose through colonialism. Christianity is also often accused of promoting discrimination, encouraging gender inequality, creating barriers to scientific progress, and standing in the way of sexual freedom. In many ways, it's the case that the actual opposite is true, but the attempted defense often appears to fall on deaf ears.

In view of this sense of tension that exists between Christianity and postmodernism, or between Christians and popular culture, or between the church and the world of our time, it is important to be realistic about some of the large challenges that the church and Christianity face in today's world. These challenges arise in various forms—some in the context of social relationships, and others on the level of philosophy or politics. Because our most immediate encounters with postmodernism happen on a social level, let me begin by detailing some of the challenges facing Christianity from that perspective.

Tolerance

I mentioned tolerance earlier as one of the prime features of postmodernism. It is based on the idea that no religious view should be regarded as being better than another. Because Christians generally feel confident that Christianity has a strong reasonable and philosophical foundation, it isn't long before their claim about the uniqueness of the Christian message is sharply challenged in the public sphere by the prevailing purveyors of postmodernism.

For example, Christian parents may face this challenge in the sphere of public education. Public education is strongly committed to the idea of individual rights based on the Charter of Rights and Freedoms adopted by the Canadian government. As mentioned earlier, the Charter makes it clear that no one should be discriminated against based on several rights, including a couple of primary interest to Christians—religion and sexual orientation. Christians would certainly agree with the premise that all people have a right to their own religious beliefs, as well as to ideas about sexual identity and expression. And they unquestionably are grateful for the protection of their own religious convictions under the Charter. The difficulty for Christians arises when they feel they are compelled to submit to the idea of pluralism in their children's exposure to public education. Even though Christians are obliged to express tolerance towards those who have different views about sexual identity, for example, they do not feel free to approve of homosexuality, bisexuality, and transgendered practice.

In postmodern society, disapproval on principles of biblical conviction is often regarded not only as intolerance, but also as discrimination, bigotry, racism, or fear. In the latter case, Christians who hold to biblical principles are often accused of "being phobic," thus having a serious psychological problem of one kind or another. In that way, Christians are maligned and do not feel free to express convictions that represent a contrary point of view. Without that freedom of expression, they feel victimized in an odd case of what may easily be described as reverse discrimination, because they are accused of being "intolerant."

The challenge in this instance is for Christians to exercise care and compassion towards those with whom, on matters of biblical principle, they strongly disagree. One response is to go with the strong biblical emphasis on love and avoid making an issue out of the matter, but love in that case seems to lack the authenticity of also being combined with truth.

Another response is to accept the new expression as status quo and then seek to find a means by which the Bible may somehow legitimately approve. Sometimes the conclusion will be that the Bible is unable to speak to what some regard as the scientific developments of the day, thus seriously undermining any true sense of biblical authority.

A third answer is to lovingly and courteously seek to explain the reason for the biblical conviction which one holds. In that case, a positive apologetic or defense based on what the Bible teaches about God's plan and purpose for sexual difference, or for the legitimate expression of it within the confines of a life-long marriage relationship between a man and a woman, must be provided. In the end, it is a matter of meeting the challenge of mindless tolerance with grace and truth. Even so, it's often unlikely that Christians will be successful in avoiding the accusation of intolerance. However, there is a great need for Christians to do due diligence in preparing to articulate these convictions with great wisdom and strength.

Another instance in which Christians may have to face the charge of intolerance is in the context of their own church life community. Again, the appeal will be to be more inclusive of people whose ideas and practices may be quite different from the church's traditional approach. Inclusiveness, of course, is just another face of tolerance. The critical element here for the church concerns the question of who is allowed to participate in communion, baptism, and membership, as well as in various roles of ministry leadership. Consider the instance of a young couple who are co-habiting without having formalized their relationship through a marriage covenant and who wish to be accepted into the full life of the church community through baptism and communion. The postmodern mindset would tend to ignore this structure of formality (marriage) as a pre-requisite to a sexual union, especially if the couple had demonstrated a significant level of commitment to one another otherwise. In such a case, the pressure upon the leaders of the church would be to exercise tolerance, perhaps justifying such for reasons of "grace" as perceived in the New Testament.

One approach may be to revisit the idea of what the Bible actually means by marriage, and whether a formal agreement is necessary as a qualification for marriage. Another emerging attitude in this situation could be that it isn't anyone's business what kind of relationship people have with one another outside of the church, as long as they are willing to confess their faith. But according to a biblical standard, this response blatantly misses the point. Another example might be of people who want to participate in the communion of the church who have unorthodox, or even cultic, theological views about Christianity. Such people could have notions that cause them to lean towards New Age ideas or practices of spirituality rooted more in the Eastern religions than New Testament Christianity.

Depending on how the church responds to these kinds of challenges, it may easily be regarded as too discriminatory and intolerant. Sometimes by communicating standards of acceptance at all, Christians might easily be labelled in ways that have racial overtones. How should the church deal with this kind of challenge?

It seems to me that it is important for Christians in these circumstances to affirm what's possible in the postmodern context while once again compassionately and patiently explaining the biblical rationale behind the standards that have been established otherwise. Too often the temptation in these situations is to accommodate the aberration in the name of grace and compassion instead of combining genuine love and care with good biblical explanation.

Orthodoxy

In his book, *A Generous Orthodoxy*, Brian McLaren plays liberally with the tension that exists between the commitment to Christian orthodoxy in the modern period and the disinterest in dogma in these postmodern times. As a typical postmodern, he quite readily admits, "… that there are places [in the book] where I have gone out of my way to be provocative, mischievous, and unclear…"[33] Further, he writes:

> …I don't mind if you think I'm wrong. I'm sure
> I am wrong about many things, although I'm not
> sure exactly which things I'm wrong about. I'm
> even sure I'm wrong about what I think I'm right
> about in at least some cases.[34]

---

33 Brian McLaren, *A Generous Orthodoxy* (El Cajon, CA: Youth Specialties, 2004), 23.

34 Ibid., 20.

In this confession of both provocativeness and uncertainty, McLaren illustrates the nature of a crucial postmodern challenge to Christianity that involves its commitment to certain theological truths. In doing so, and to some degree to his credit, McLaren is reflecting a desire to relinquish theological dogma for the sake of, from his perspective, encouraging a relationship with Jesus. Postmodernism has a bias against belief that does not result in practice. In other words, it is no use making a confession of faith in Christ if one does not authenticate the confession through true obedience to Christ. Again and again, postmoderns will land on Jesus' strong condemnation of the Pharisees for having all kinds of rules based on their peculiar theology that not only falsely justified their idea of righteousness, but also made a huge display of their blatant hypocrisy. The problem with the church, in the postmodern view, is that it is too much like the Pharisees.

Therefore, one of the challenges with which the church of these times needs to contend is this critique of its obsession with doctrine at the expense of the kind of compassion that seems more characteristic of the ministry of Jesus. In actual experience, this difference shows up in various controversies having to do with belief and practice. One current issue in the Canadian evangelical church, for example, concerns gender roles. Those with a mindset peculiar to the modern period will tend to be more inclined towards insisting that there is a significant distinction in scripture between the roles of men and women in marriage as well as in the leadership of the church. Based on a more traditional hermeneutical approach to the understanding of scripture, they will seek to show that God has called men to roles of leadership in marriage and the church, while women are called to roles of support.

Of course, such a conclusion is not well received by post-moderns for more reasons than one. In the first place, they have a predisposition to be inclusive rather than exclusive. They are opposed to what they believe have been superficial distinctions that mitigate any sense of equality. Sometimes they accuse modernists of promoting the politics of division, both in the church and otherwise. This reference to the politics of division is a frequent expression in today's popular culture. For example, in campaigning before the last Canadian election, it was common to hear one party accusing the other of the politics of division.

A second reason why postmoderns oppose a complementarian view of gender is because they don't think the subject even deserves air-time. They would say that Jesus was not concerned with those kinds of issues. His focus, rather, was on the mission of spreading the good news of the kingdom. It's one of the reasons postmoderns appear to have a special interest in the Gospels in contrast to the Epistles of Paul and the apostles. Jesus' call to discipleship, they would say, was about active obedience to Christ in his work of mission, not about discussions on theological issues, least of all about the roles of men and women in the church. Sure, they would say, he chose twelve *men* to be his personal disciples, but that simply reflected the culture of the times in which he lived; it was not a principled decision.

This kind of conflict tends also to characterize other kinds of potential disagreement, such as ecclesiology (the nature of church government), eschatology (views on prophetic events related to Christ's second coming), sanctification (the doctrine of holiness), ordination (what constitutes a call to professional ministry), and even matters related to the specifics of salvation, baptism, and church membership. About a decade ago, much of this kind of debate took place in the context of discussion concerning what came to be called, "the emergent church."

There is much in this recent emergent church movement that reflects quite well what postmodernism is all about. Though as a movement by that name, the emergent church is virtually dead, various ideas from within that movement are still common. As a movement, the emergent church tried to modify the terms of reference concerning the church and orthodoxy in the way that Brian McLaren writes about it his book. Donald Carson makes this point in his book, *Becoming Conversant with the Emerging Church*.

> At the heart of the "movement" … lies the conviction that changes in the culture signal that a new church is "emerging." Christian leaders must therefore adapt to this emerging church. Those who fail to do so are blind to the cultural accretions that hide the gospel behind forms of thought and modes of expression that no longer communicate with the new generation, the emerging generation.[35]

Carson goes on to describe this emerging movement in terms of the difference between modernism and postmodernism.

> Modernism is often pictured as pursuing truth, absolutism, linear thinking, rationalism, certainty, the cerebral as opposed to the affective—which in turn breeds arrogance, inflexibility, a lust to be right, the desire to control. Postmodernism, by contrast, recognizes that how much of what we "know" is shaped by the culture in which we live,

---

35 D. A. Carson, *Becoming Conversant with the Emerging Church* (Grand Rapids, MI: Zondervan, 2005), 2.

is controlled by emotions and aesthetics and heritage, and in fact can only be intelligently held as part of a common tradition, without overbearing claims to being true or right.[36]

It's easy to see, when it comes to the matter of orthodoxy, why there is such a strong sense of tension and potential conflict between moderns and postmoderns. Postmoderns take a whole different approach to understanding orthodoxy. They each have a different approach to hermeneutics regarding the understanding of biblical thought. I will discuss the hermeneutical issue forthwith, but for now, suffice it to say that postmoderns talk a lot about understanding the ethos (the cultural factors of the time) in which a biblical passage occurred. For example, they would tend to say that the stronger references, especially in the Old Testament, to male leadership are simply a reflection of the culture of the time, and not necessarily a true representation of God's principled intention for the nature of the relationship between men and women.

Moderns, on the other hand, are inclined to push back in favour of what they would consider a more vigorous orthodoxy that has a lot to say about the respective distinct roles of men and women in marriage and in church leadership. In general, moderns believe that the issue ultimately concerns a stronger conviction and view about the importance of biblical authority, about biblical inerrancy and thus, a more traditional hermeneutical approach. That approach guarantees that context and historical references in the Bible are given important consideration; but it also means that special attention is given to the nature, meaning, and order of the words, especially within the framework of their original use.

---

36   Ibid., 27.

With these considerations in mind, a couple of millennial writers, Kevin DeYoung and Ted Kluck, have written about their response to the emergent church movement in their book, *Why We're Not Emergent*.

> The first problem with the emergent view of journey is that it undermines the knowability of God. Theologians have long held to God's knowability along with his immensity ... But emergent leaders are allowing the immensity of God to swallow up His knowability. In good postmodern fashion, they are questioning whether we can have any real, accurate knowledge about God in the first place.[37]

They go on to state:

> The God of the Bible is nothing if He is not a God who speaks to His people. To be sure, none of us ever infinitely understand God in a nice, neat package of affirmations and denials, but we can know him truly, both personally and propositionally. God can speak. He can use human language to communicate truth about Himself that is accurate and knowable, without ceasing to be God because we've somehow got Him all figured out.[38]

In my view, this illustrates the great difference and tension between moderns and postmoderns in the context of today's church

---

37 Kevin DeYoung and Ted Kluck, *Why We're Not Emergent* (Chicago: Moody Publishers, 2008), 35.

38 Ibid., 37.

experience. That difference is largely about theological orthodoxy and especially about what the church has traditionally believed concerning the role of scripture in defining what we believe vis-à-vis the ideas that emerge through postmodern philosophy (or any other religion or philosophy for that matter). Granted, it is not merely a matter of holding orthodox views blindly, or without having them tested with the best of biblical scholarship in the context of the real world. But it does mean that Christians need to know the difference between these views and how to engage their own view of orthodoxy with the broader culture in a manner that also demonstrates respect for people of differing views.

Judgementalism

It is soon obvious in considering the various challenges that Christianity and the church face in relation to postmodernism that there is a good deal of overlap between various issues. It would be quite possible to speak of these challenges from a variety of perspectives. One of the most pressing challenges confronting Christians is the charge of being extremely judgemental. This charge is not surprising considering the emphasis on tolerance and inclusiveness in postmodernism, but since judgement is a word that often comes up in current discussion on a variety of subjects, it's worth considering as a separate issue.

Earlier I mentioned a newspaper editorial that offered a scathing rebuke of a Christian camp that sought to qualify a potential leader based on her beliefs, particularly her apparent approval of homosexuality. Being a Christian Bible camp, its policy in this instance was that staff were to avoid conduct that is unethical or immoral or contrary to biblical principles, including premarital and extramarital sexual relations, as well as homosexuality. The editorial goes on to quote extensively from the Gospels about love, about being a servant (Mark 10:43–44), and about not judging others (quoting Luke 6:37 and 7:3). The editorial amounted to a kind of "sermon," especially for the camp (and for Christians in general), which was a bit ironic considering the source. However, it illustrates the strong theme in today's postmodern world that Christians are in no position to judge others.

This charge against Christians as being judgemental is a classic case of the clash of the two cultures—Christianity and postmodernism. Postmoderns are easily offended by Christian allusions to biblical righteousness, because fundamentally postmoderns are strongly opposed to anyone's claim to higher knowledge or insight, especially in the matter of morality. Postmoderns are offended because they deny the Christian metanarrative of God's creation and control in the world, which would imply individual and corporate accountability to him. They are offended by the slightest suggestion that they may be wrong about their perspective. They have bought into the postmodern philosophy that all truth claims are false, because they truly believe such claims cannot be substantiated. In their view, historical documents (such as the biblical one) cannot be trusted, because in one way or another, they are often used as a means of social control.

In view of this perspective, it's easy to see why postmoderns react to any attempt by another person or group to offer censorship. The irony in the charge of being judgemental regarding some issue of morality is that postmoderns use the biblical reference to give weight to their own accusation. Additionally, as in the case of the editorial, they are inclined to lump all Christians in with the Pharisees, whom Jesus judged as being self-righteous. In doing so, they appear to be blind to the inconsistency in their own form of judgement and self-righteousness. They often justify their reaction by citing the many instances of Christian hypocrisy which, of course, cannot always be denied.

Often the charge that Christians are judgemental is spoken of in terms of the more serious accusation of discrimination, which carries the connotation of prejudice towards others because of age, race, sex, or some other status that is considered innate or uncontrollable. Sometimes they are even charged with xenophobia—an irrational fear of that which is strange or foreign, often applied to the fear of people from a foreign culture. While Christians would agree in principle that discrimination related to any natural kind of status is wrong, they may sometimes disagree on what may be regarded as someone's natural status. For example, since there is no substantiated evidence to support the claim that one's disposition towards the practice of homosexuality is innate, and since the practice is biblically censored both in the Old and New Testaments, Christians do not feel it is discriminatory to speak out against homosexuality. Though they are called to uphold the law regarding discrimination, as well as biblically called to be compassionate towards those who struggle with homosexual desire or any other moral wrong, they will seek to find ways for such persons to overcome it, ultimately through the gospel of Jesus Christ.

It certainly is the case that Christians can be judgemental in the ways that Jesus strictly condemned. The problem of judging others by moral law is a universal tendency. According to the Bible (Romans 2:15), everyone is intuitively aware of God's laws as these have been made explicit in the Ten Commandments given to Israel through Moses. That is the reason why instances of judgement are so prolific in social relationships of every description, in the secular culture and in the news media.

Everyone knows instinctively that it is wrong to disrespect one's parents, to lie, to steal, to kill, and to commit adultery. In pointing this out in the Sermon on the Mount in Matthew 5–7, Jesus made it clear that these can occur first as thoughts and attitudes of the heart, and only secondarily as actions. Everyone tends to judge other people by that intuitive standard of God's righteousness and its various corollaries. Saint Paul's main point in Romans 2, particularly as it applies to the Jews in that passage, is that they will be judged by the same standard that they use to judge others.

Therefore, the universal difficulty when judging others is that we will be judged by the same standard. Jesus' strong words in Matthew 7:1, "*Judge not, that you be not judged*," need to be understood in that context. In typical Jewish style, Jesus' words in verse 1 are repeated appositionally in verse 2: "*For with the same judgment you pronounce you will be judged.*"

It is true that those who confess faith in Christ and profess to follow him know intuitively and explicitly that they are called to a high standard of inner and practical righteousness that makes their judgement of others a very serious matter. They may rightfully be accused of hypocrisy to the extent that they themselves do not live by what they preach. To be sure, this is not an uncommon tendency among Christians—to live ingenuously while yet judging others in corresponding issues. However, it's important to recognize the huge difference between affirming the truth of God's law in various ways and being hypocritical about obedience to it. The two should not be considered mutually exclusive. It's possible to be very familiar with God's law and also to speak of its universal application. The difficulty is in making a specific application to others without reference to one's own need for grace from God in how it is to be applied.

It's certainly true that Christians need to be careful about making judgements that discredit the value of any person, but that shouldn't preclude the possibility and responsibility of speaking about the biblical expression of any transgression of God's law. As in the case cited earlier, the Christian camp is perfectly within its legal and ethical right to teach and uphold a standard regarding sexual behaviour that it feels is biblical. The challenge is to demonstrate the reasonableness of that code of conduct and to apply it consistently without making a value statement about any person who holds a contrary view.

Hermeneutics

As alluded to earlier, another significant area of potential conflict between Christianity and postmodernism concerns the matter of hermeneutics, because hermeneutics involves the meaning of words and how they are used in any particular case, whether it be in text or speech. Most often hermeneutics concerns textual analysis, especially ancient texts such as the Bible. Since a major element of postmodernism concerns the way language is used, and how it professes to create reality, interpretation is a big issue in these times.

The great theologian Thomas Aquinas is said to have inferred that it is the task of the philosopher to make distinctions. What Aquinas meant is that truth is dependent upon the ability to discern—the capability to distinguish "this" from "that" in the realm of knowledge. However, if objective and absolute truth does not exist, as postmodernism implies, then everything becomes a matter of personal interpretation. To the postmodern person, the author of a book does not possess the correct interpretation of their work; it is the reader who actually determines what the book means through a process called deconstruction. Deconstruction challenges the idea that words have a standard or common meaning. Multiple readers mean that there can be multiple interpretations with the ultimate result of no universally valid interpretation.

Such a chaotic situation makes it impossible to establish meaningful or lasting distinctions between interpretations, because there is no standard or benchmark that can be used. This especially applies to matters of faith and religion, because the philosophers of the Enlightenment and modernism have already deposed religion to the compartment of opinion. That being the case, it naturally follows that attempts to make proper and meaningful distinctions in the matter of religion (daring to suggest that one belief is more accurate than another) carries no more weight than one person arguing that chocolate tastes better than vanilla. In such situations, it becomes impossible to objectively adjudicate between competing truth claims.

The confusion concerning interpretation is especially evident in the larger church body in general, but certainly also in the evangelical church to which I belong. For one thing, it seems evident that many pastors today have departed from what was once known as expositional preaching. This was an approach to preaching in which the sermon expounded on the meaning of the words or phrases in a text or passage, according to the best possible means of understanding the original words in their historical, grammatical and cultural context. Typically, the sermon made applications to life based on that kind of exposition. This approach, somewhat peculiar to the modern period, was based on the idea that God's intention could be clearly known in the words and contexts that were used. This kind of preaching also made a lot out of biblical inerrancy, meaning that the Bible was without error in its original scripting through the actual writers of the text.

Most evangelical pastors today, at least by profession, continue to maintain a commitment to the idea of biblical inerrancy. In doing so, they also continue to hold strongly to the concept of biblical authority that is so vital to preaching, not to mention the spiritual life and progress of the church community. However, expositional preaching itself has sometimes given way to less precise ways of analyzing the language of scripture, or of considering a meaning that suits one's perspective. In these postmodern times, it is often likely that the kind of sermon the average parishioner hears will be more of a thematic or narrative nature. Some attention may be given to the general context of the passage, but the emphasis will tend to be on demonstrating how the passage itself fits into the larger narrative of scripture while also being relevant to today's human story. This is based on the postmodern idea that we can't necessarily know the original context or the intent of the actual writers of the text; therefore, we cannot have the same level of certainty of the meaning of the words used.

A couple of authors writing for the *Journal of the Evangelical Theological Society* have described the situation well:

> Some among us have become relative relativists, yielding more and more ground to the realm of uncertainty. In our endeavor to be honest about our own preunderstanding and fallibility, and increasingly uncertain about human ability to say words that correspond with reality, we retreat from defending historic understandings of difficult texts to defending important teaching that has clear (unambiguous, repeated) biblical authority. Then we retreat again from defending those to defending with conviction only the major tenets

of the Christian faith. When we gave up holy kisses and head coverings, no one worried. When we gave up washing feet and silent women, some folks winced a little. Now we are challenged by fellow evangelicals to give up Adam and Eve, role distinctions in marriage, limitations on divorce, exclusively heterosexual unions, hell, faith in Jesus Christ as the only way to acceptance with God and—most pivotal—an inerrant Bible. On this last point, some declare themselves to be "limited inerrantists," which means, I take it, that passages without error are limited to those sanctioned by the interpreter. This undermining of Biblical authority does not all stem from postmodern thinking, of course, but postmodern ways of thinking have softened us up to accept what otherwise might not even be entertained.[39]

As illustrated, this lack of certainty about texts and words means that pastors tend to stay clear of passages that are more theologically controversial, such as matters relating to gender distinctions, prophetic events, and holy living, to name a few. However, it should be noted that this new approach to preaching is also partly because pastoral leaders seek more for inclusion rather than division. They truly believe that many of the distinctions that a former generation made, in theology and the interpretation of the Bible, that also led to denominational identities and differences,

---

39 Robertson McQuilkin and Bradford Mullen, "The Impact of Post-Modern Thinking on Evangelical Hermeneutics," *Journal of the Evangelical Theological Society*, 40 no. 1 (March 1997), 71.

were superficial and unnecessary. This, no doubt, is a large reason
for the apparent change in approaches to pastoral ministry, not to
mention ecumenism.

The change in homiletical preaching is most certainly due to a
significant degree of change in the way the language of scripture is
analyzed and understood. One of the possible effects of this change
is that more attention is given to how changes in the culture of our
times fit with scripture. In other words, the great temptation in
these times is to try to make the Bible say what is more palatable
to existing culture. In the modern period, this practice, considered
a grave error, was known as eisegesis. It entailed imposing one's
own ideas (also often with strong biases) upon a text instead of
allowing the text to speak for itself, regardless of the judgements or
applications it may bring forward.

On the other hand, postmoderns would likely contend that
moderns had their own biases in coming to the text. Or, they might
say, it's impossible to know the original intent of the text, because
its meaning can't help but be eroded by the passage of time and by
our understanding of the meaning of the words in their original
context. Therefore, in line with deconstruction, the new approach
to the interpretation of scripture is to not worry so much about
the words of the original language, but to try to imagine and then,
quite possibly, to impose one's own ideas about the words and
applications of the time.

Another emphasis in postmodernism, potentially very helpful,
is to pay attention to the literary genre of the text being considered.
Poetic language and passages of the Bible like the Psalms cannot
always be considered in the most literal use of the words. Psalm
23 speaks of the Lord being one's shepherd and his leading "*beside
still waters and green pastures*." Unless one is thinking in terms of a

camping experience, it's obvious in the language and the context that the writer is speaking metaphorically.

Historical and narrative language, characteristic of many of the books of the Old Testament and the Gospels, needs to be treated literally, though they are filled with practical and spiritual lessons that ultimately point to the significance of the coming of Jesus Christ. Other passages of the Bible were written as law for the Jewish people of a certain time, as in the case of much of Leviticus and Deuteronomy. In them we would look for principles of God's moral law (which are also emphasized in the New Testament). It is understood in those Old Testament laws that God's intention for Christians today is not for their literal application, since many of them held a ceremonial purpose that has now, it is understood, been fulfilled in Christ (Matthew 5:17).

The Epistles of the New Testament, most of which were written by the apostles or original disciples of Christ, also are a unique genre of biblical literature. Prepared for particular churches of that time yet with universal application for all succeeding generations of Christians, they consist of explanations and exhortations regarding doctrines. It is true that some exhortations have peculiar cultural relevance, such as greeting one another with a holy kiss, or of women wearing a head-covering while in church assembly. Yet, even then, some would contend that these references have principled innuendos. But for the most part, the Christian church has always understood the practical exhortations of the Epistles to be applicable today.

One of the biggest challenges in hermeneutics centers on the understanding and application of biblical literature that is deemed prophetic and apocalyptic. Prophetic literature is often poetic and figurative. Most often in the biblical context, it had relevance to particular peoples and places and concerned God's judgements or blessings, but also his plans and purposes through future events. Many prophecies in the Old Testament seemed to have had both an immediate as well as a future fulfillment. Take, for example, the case of the prophecy to Israel's King Ahaz concerning God's gift of a sign that a virgin would conceive and bear a son (Isaiah 7:14). The prophecy had an immediate application, no doubt, but Christians have always believed that it is a very specific prophecy concerning the nature of Jesus' supernatural conception because of how it is applied by Matthew in his Gospel (Matthew 1:23).

There are spiritual principles in these prophecies that have meaning for our lives today, but it also seems evident that some of the prophecies of the Old Testament represent God's plan for fulfillment in our times or even in the future. Consider Daniel's prophecies, for example, concerning "seventy weeks" (9:24) until the time of the end, or Jesus' prophetic words concerning the destruction of the temple and the "abomination of desolation" (Matthew 24:15), or Paul's writings concerning the "coming of the Lord" (1 Thessalonians 4:13–18). *Apocalyptic* is a special kind of prophecy that has to do with the revelation of God's coming judgement upon the world as described in the book of Revelation. Again, it's true that we need to consider the use of figurative language, versus what will literally take place. These are difficult distinctions, especially in postmodern times because of questions about the meaning and contextual use of words. But through the best of biblical research, these distinctions are not impossible.

Evangelical Christians (and others) differ about many issues, especially during this postmodern period. While general agreement on the authority of the Bible exists in the sense that it stands as God's written revelation to humankind, understanding the words and how they might be applied is another matter. In this postmodern period, there is less confidence about God's intention in the words, about how they were understood and received by the original human writers and audience, and about how their original meaning can successfully be transferred to today's readers and audience. Therefore, it's not surprising that pastors in these times often speak with less confidence about the nature of the gospel, evangelism, church life and ministry, gender distinctions, matters concerning sexual morality, and prophetic events.

One example of special interest in these times is the issue of the roles of men and women in church ministry. More than many other current issues, this illustrates how postmoderns tend to interpret the Bible differently from moderns. Key texts concerning the roles of men and women include Genesis 1—3, John 20:1-18, Acts 2:17—18, Romans 16:1, 1 Corinthians 11:1–16, 1 Corinthians 14:34–35, Galatians 3:28, Ephesians 5:22–33, 1 Timothy 2:11–15, 1 Timothy 3:1–7, and 1 Peter 3:1–7.

Those who argue for the position of no distinctions between women and men, both in marriage and in church leadership, are most often spoken of as egalitarians, or egals (speaking of equality in their relationship to one another). Those who defend a distinction in which women are called to a complementary role in relation to men – especially in marriage and church leadership – speak of those who hold this view as complementarians, or comps. Both would agree, based on Genesis 1:27, that God created women and men to share equally in life and the management of God's world. Complementarians, however, make much of the fact that, based on Genesis 2 in the actual details of his creation, God created the woman from the man as a "helper" for him in the work that God has called him to do.

Egalitarians, on the other hand, are inclined to think of the Hebrew word for "helper" not as a word referring to support, but as a word reflecting assistance, in the same sense of the many instances in which the word is used of God as a helper for his people. But that view seems to beg the question since it gives the impression that a wife has God's divine ability to help. Both would acknowledge that the results of the Fall in Genesis 3 came initially because of Eve's temptation through the speaking serpent to have the wisdom of God. Egals believe that the consequence of disobedience for her was not her ambition to be like her husband, but that he would have dominion over her. They believe that this resulted in the patriarchal society, which is supremely evident throughout the entire Old Testament, not only in the choices of leaders, but also in the service of the tabernacle and temple. Further, they feel that this "inequality" resulting from the Fall has been overcome in Christ's victory over sin.

Complementarians, on the other hand, think that the Genesis account, in the actual creation of men and women, reflects a legitimate sense of role distinction which the Fall, contrary to God's intention in the original creation, served to exacerbate into extremes. Consider that egalitarians generally believe that the Old Testament was written in the context of a strong patriarchal society that resulted from the sin of Adam and Eve in the Garden. In that sense, egalitarians think this needs to be borne in mind when considering the writings of the Old Testament. Complementarians, on the other hand, think that the patriarchal nature of the Old Testament reflects God's basic intention regarding the role distinction between men and women (while yet agreeing with the idea of uncomfortable tensions between the two sexes caused by the Fall). They both would agree that neither the Fall nor God's design precluded the evident possibility of women (as demonstrated by Miriam, Naomi, Ruth, Abigail, Esther, and Huldah), rising to places of great honour by God's design, or by necessity, like Deborah (because men were unwilling to lead).

Egalitarians point to the John passage about Mary being chosen as the first witness to the resurrection of Christ, or the Acts 2 passage as proof that God has poured out his Spirit indiscriminately on both men and women. Complementarians, on the other hand, would contend that Mary's initial witness to Jesus' resurrection signifies his regard for women in general, but doesn't necessarily set a precedent for church leadership. And the Acts passage needs to be considered in the context of the whole revelation of God concerning this subject. Comps would agree that women may also be given roles of prophecy but that such gifting doesn't displace the principle mentioned in other biblical references to male spiritual leadership in the church.

The Galatians verse (3:28) is pivotal, because it appears that God eliminates any difference between men and women through faith in Christ. However, complementarians would point out that this doesn't seem to include the sense of role distinction to which Paul and the apostles allude in other passages, such as Ephesians 5, Colossians 3:18–22, and 1 Peter 3:1–7, or the ones in Paul's instructions to churches (1 Corinthians 11:2-16; 1 Timothy 2, 3). Complementarians believe that the context of Galatians 3:28 points to the fact that there is no difference between men and women regarding their common blessings of redemption in Christ; it doesn't speak to differences in roles, which is set forth in the other passages cited here.

Interpretation becomes an even bigger issue in the way each approaches the text of 1 Corinthians 11 and 14 and the one in 1 Timothy 2. Egalitarians are inclined to say that these references are not universally applicable, because they were merely written for specific churches at that time. In other words, they contend, these passages need to be interpreted with the immediate situation in mind. The Corinthian passage, according to egalitarians, obviously reflects something of the culture of that time in general, which dictated that a woman of honour should wear a head covering, especially in the context of worship. The specific reference in 1 Corinthians 14:34–35 concerning women keeping silent in church, egalitarians would say, was a cultural adaptation.

Complementarians would generally agree about the relevance of cultural elements, but still consider that the principle of male leadership to which these passages allude needs to be upheld. For example, they might contend that the directive concerning a woman's head covering is satisfied by her generally longer hair; women's silence, perhaps, as a more subdued voice in deference to their husbands or men in general. Likewise, in the case of 1 Timothy 2, egalitarians think that Paul's letter to Timothy had to do with a unique issue for the church in Ephesus, where he was pastor, in which certain women were promoting false teaching and overstepping their bounds ("usurping authority"). Others with that perspective think that Paul is speaking about some wives who were mean-spirited in how they were taking authority over their husbands. Considering the whole context, complementarians think the language has more of a universal application, since it also refers to a certain order in the creation of Adam and Eve, as well as to Eve's initial experience of deception (by Satan) instead of Adam's.

Other arguments involving approaches to interpretation are made on both sides of this debate. Egalitarians commonly refer to a good number of instances both in the Old and New Testaments in which it seems evident that God employed women in critical roles of leadership, such as Priscilla (Acts 18) and Phoebe (Romans 1:16). Based on a consistent grammatical, historical, and contextual hermeneutic, complementarians would argue that although there are significant instances of women in various levels of influence and leadership, the Bible generally seems to make a distinction between how men and women can best fulfill their God-given, honourable roles both in marriage (Ephesians 5) and the church (1 Timothy 2, 3, and Titus). They would also affirm that while the basic principle of role distinctions should be upheld, there is a good deal of latitude in scripture about how these distinctions might be applied. Generally, the distinction in a marriage and church context, from the perspective of Christian decorum, has more to do with the issue of spiritual authority. Complementarians contend that the Bible leads us to conclude that God has given a special responsibility for spiritual leadership to men. That is why they insist that the lay leaders (elders) and lead pastors of the church should be men.

The matter of gender roles is a good illustration of a current major difference in the church due to different approaches in interpretation. Many other examples might be cited in which various hermeneutical approaches appear to be extensions of the philosophical divide between moderns and postmoderns.

Hopefully this helps the reader understand why these kinds of tensions exist in the church today, and how popular culture influences biblical hermeneutics. The question of gender roles was seldom a point of debate during the modern era, at least in the context of church life and ministry, but postmodern thinking has contributed significantly, for example, to the rise of feminism, to the point of obliterating valid role distinctions. Unfortunately, the issue has been reduced to a simple matter of discrimination. Yet it must also be conceded that this reaction (often an emotional one) is partially due, no doubt, to the kinds of abuses that have occurred frequently towards women throughout human history and also during the modern period. In actual fact, it is evident that the gospel of the New Testament restores men and women to their honourable distinctive roles which God intended from the time of creation.

Perhaps the most critical subject of all in the matter of hermeneutics concerns the biblical definition of "the gospel." As the New
Testament states, it is by means of this gospel that we are saved
(1 Corinthians 15:2). Paul refers often to the gospel and takes
great pains to ensure that his readers understand the true nature
of that gospel. The shortened version of that gospel, according to
1 Corinthians 15:3–4, concerns the death, burial, and resurrection
of Jesus Christ. Paul's longer theological definition of the gospel is
given to us in his letter to the Romans. The theme of the letter is
set out in Romans 1:16–17, where he speaks of the gospel as "*the
power of God for salvation to everyone who believes*," because through
it we learn that the "*righteousness of God*" is obtained by faith.
Succeeding passages of the Epistle go on to explain that this is so
because no one can be adequately righteous through trying to keep
God's law. The absolute righteousness that God requires is only
possible through faith in Jesus Christ, who God provided as a "*pro-
pitiation by his blood*" (Romans 3:25) for the judgement of sin over
all our lives. Paul goes on to make the point that he's talking about
a very genuine kind of faith that is demonstrated through a verbal
confession (Romans 10:9–10), but also through ongoing trust and
obedience that is truly life-changing (Romans 6, 12).

There have always been those who have tried to make a distinction between what they perceive as Paul's version of the
gospel versus James', for example. But the apparent difference is
resolved in James' frequent call to a genuine faith that is shown
in radical obedience. In recent years, there have been those who
also seek to make a distinction between Jesus' version of the gospel
and Paul's. Again, if we believe that the Bible is consistent with
itself, this distinction is invalid, for it can be shown that Jesus' good
news of the kingdom was really about entering into a life of faith
in his supreme lordship—something quite impossible without also

acknowledging and receiving his forgiveness of sin. Yet there are those who believe the meaning of the gospel has been distorted by an over-emphasis on soteriology or salvation, at the expense of understanding the gospel as a call to discipleship. Once again, it's a matter of hermeneutics.

This latter version is the approach taken by Scot McKnight in his book, *The King Jesus Gospel*. He writes:

> My plea is that we go back to the New Testament to discover all over again what the Jesus gospel is and that by embracing it we become true evangelicals ... What has happened is that we have created a "salvation culture" and mistakenly assumed it is a "gospel culture."[40]

Essentially, McKnight believes that a former generation understood the gospel incorrectly, or at least incompletely. He doesn't use the words "modern" or "postmodern," but (perhaps unwittingly) he challenges the modern notion in which he assumes that the gospel was only about individual salvation. His modified view, based on what he feels is a deeper reading of the Bible, especially the New Testament, is that the gospel is the completion of the story of Israel in which Jesus is introduced as the Messiah. The implication, for him, is that the gospel is about much more than mere salvation; it is about receiving and following Christ as King.

> There is a Person at the very core of the gospel of Paul, and until that Person is put into the center of centers in Paul's gospel, we will not comprehend

---

40 Scot McKnight, *The King Jesus Gospel: The Original Good News Revisited* (Grand Rapids: Zondervan Pub, 2011), 29.

> ... the apostles' gospel accurately. The gospel
> Story of Jesus Christ is a story about Jesus as
> Messiah, Jesus as Lord, Jesus as Savior, and Jesus
> as Son.[41]

McKnight contends that the gospel of evangelicalism in the past has been too simplistic, and that it didn't really express very well the idea of the completion of the Israel story in Jesus' coming as the promised Messiah who now invites believers into the experience and requirements of what it means to live as his kingdom people. He believes the gospel is misrepresented and falls short of God's intention if it merely emphasizes Jesus' substitutionary atonement. Furthermore, he believes that this is the gospel that Jesus preached in the Gospels and that Paul and the apostles preached in their sermons in Acts.

Another writer, N. T. Wright, who provides one of the "Forewords" to McKnight's book, makes a similar claim concerning the nature of the gospel. He too says it is not so much about the future, since we know so little about it (a rather typical postmodern conclusion). It's more about experiencing the resurrection life of Jesus now and participating in his mission to inaugurate his kingdom.

> ...the gospel, in the New Testament, is the good
> news that God (the world's creator) is at last
> becoming king and that Jesus, whom this God
> raised from the dead, is the world's true lord ...
> The power of the gospel lies not in the offer of
> a new spirituality or religious experience, not in
> the threat of hellfire ... which can be removed if
> only the hearer checks this box, says this prayer,

---

41 McKnight, 55.

raises a hand, or whatever, but in the powerful
announcement that God is God, that Jesus is
Lord, that the powers of evil have been defeated
and that God's new world has begun.[42]

Clearly, both McKnight and Wright interpret the gospel of the
New Testament in ways that are somewhat different from evangelical Christians have known in the past. Probably it's fair to say
that the former emphasis on the gospel as Jesus' atonement for our
sins is more in keeping with what we recognize as a Reformed (or
Reformation) view of the gospel, well represented in recent days
by John Piper. He is an articulate proponent of the gospel as justification before God by faith in the atonement and resurrection of
Jesus Christ. Piper writes:

> The doctrine of justification says that the remedy
> for my alienation from God is first a legal one, and
> only then a moral one. First, I have to be legally
> absolved of guilt and credited with a righteous-
> ness that I don't have ... To make a way for us to
> be saved, God sent Christ to live a perfect divine
> human life and die an obedient death. In this way
> Christ became the substitute punishment for our
> sins ... and the substitute performer of our righ-
> teousness ... I am declared just—freed from the
> punishment of sin and now possessing a title to
> heaven. This is what we mean by justification.[43]

---

42 N. T. Wright, *Surprised by Hope: Rethinking Heaven, the Resurrection,
   and the Mission of the Church* (New York: Harper Collins, 2008), 226.

43 John Piper, *When I Don't Desire God: How to Fight for Joy* (Wheaton, Ill:
   Crossway Books, 2004), 82.

Though the differences between these two interpretations of the gospel are somewhat compatible, they illustrate why so much of church ministry has taken a new direction. McKnight and Wright, as well as others, do not see the gospel essentially as personal justification for eternal life and salvation, but as a recognition of the coming of Christ's kingdom and alignment with his purposes regarding its inauguration. For those pastors and churches who interpret the gospel in these terms, it will greatly affect the nature of their ministries. That is why, for example, there will be less reference to evangelism in these times and much more stress on discipleship. "Discipleship," in fact, along with "mission," are the new operative words for church ministry—due largely, no doubt, to this shift in interpretation of the gospel.

It's important to recognize that this shift has not been entirely negative. It is true that "gospel" can be understood too narrowly, resulting in an "easy believism" that is no real faith at all, or involves a perspective that merely consists of escape from hell, and the prospect of eternal life in heaven. But it's possible that a strong denial of the importance of justification based on Jesus' atonement for sin can easily lead to a distortion of what the true gospel is all about. For example, if the gospel is merely the call to discipleship, how will a person who professes to be a disciple of Jesus ever know if they are being sufficiently obedient to Christ in order to have the assurance that he or she is accepted by God and belongs to God? Could such an emphasis, in fact, lead to the old danger of seeking to find ultimate acceptance with God through a system of merit – something that is foreign to the gospel of the New Testament (i.e. Ephesians 2:8, 9)?

True evangelism, it would seem, consists of the kind of communication of the gospel that emphasizes our inability to be justified before God merely by our own efforts. Rather, justification before God is only possible through a humble acknowledgment of falling short of his holy perfection, and a genuine response of faith in Jesus' atoning sacrifice for sins, which he accomplished through his death and resurrection. Biblically speaking, it seems quite clear that justification with God involves both a confession of our need for him (because of sin), repentance (or a willingness to turn from sin), and a decision to follow Jesus. In the modern era, we used to speak of these two aspects of conversion as justification and sanctification; today, it may be fine to speak of justification and discipleship, as long as we understand the difference and don't lose sight of how discipleship fits with the concept of sanctification, or true holiness—which also, according to the Bible, is by faith (Romans 6 and 7; 1 Corinthians 1:30).

The insights of McKnight, Wright, and others notwithstanding, I'd be inclined to stick with what the New Testament writers appear to be saying about the gospel as justification. The gospel is good news about the everlasting Kingdom of God and how we may enter it through a genuine confession of faith (i.e. Romans 10:9–10) that also involves repentance, new birth, and true conversion (Titus 3:4–7). I have no quarrel with the idea of the gospel also being about an ongoing discipleship relationship with Christ (which really is part of the whole gospel), but I don't think it is helpful to somehow trade that idea with all that is entailed in justification and its accompanying expressions through a confession of faith.

We could look at many other examples of how differences in the understanding and approach to biblical hermeneutics have impacted the most foundational aspects of evangelical faith, but the main point in this chapter is, that for all the benefits that come from postmodernism, there is also real potential for a significant degree of conflict—not only between Christianity and the world, but also within different parts of the church itself. It is this impasse that accounts for the challenges that confront Christians seeking to effectively "broadcast" the good news concerning Jesus, and it also accounts for the confusion that has emerged within the church. In the next chapter, I address the question of how we may effectively engage the culture of our times with the truth of the gospel, as well as how it's possible to pursue true unity in the church.

CHAPTER 8

Communicating the Good News in Postmodern Times

If there is one thing that made the nation of Israel in the Old Testament unique among its national neighbours, it was primarily their practice of worship. When God called Abram from his Chaldean roots in Ur (today's land of Iraq), his promise to begin a great nation through him included a means of blessing the whole world (Genesis 12:1–3). At that time, Israel's distinctiveness among the nations was God's self-revelation to them. Paul's answer to his rhetorical question in Romans 3:2 concerning the advantage of the Jews is that "*the Jews were entrusted with the oracles of God.*" By means of his own witness and their response, God established a covenant relationship with the Jews in which it was possible for them to acceptably worship him and experience his blessing.

At that time, the nation of Israel was set apart from the rest of the world partially to demonstrate how all the peoples of the world could ultimately experience God's blessing. In the end, despite God's best efforts through his deeds and words (by way of the prophets), the people of Israel were often unfaithful to the covenant he had established with them. As far back as the time of the judges, the Israelites had a penchant to stray drastically from the worship of Jehovah.

> And they abandoned the Lord, the God of their fathers, who had brought them out of the land of Egypt. They went after other gods, from among the gods of the peoples who were around them, and bowed down to them. And they provoked the Lord to anger. They abandoned the Lord and serve the Baals and the Ashtaroth. (Judges 2:12–13)

Again and again, God sent his prophets to speak to the people and warn them about the error of their ways.

> And they abandoned the house of the Lord, the God of their fathers, and served the Asherim and the idols. And wrath came upon Judah and Jerusalem for this guilt of theirs. Yet he sent prophets among them to bring them back to the Lord. They testified against them, but they would not pay attention. (2 Chronicles 24:18–19).

Overall, God's relationship with Israel provides an excellent picture of the Creator's relentless commitment to love and care for his people. His plan was to ultimately enable them to be the avenue by which his salvation and blessing could come to the whole world through the coming of Jesus Christ.

Through the covenant of faith and blessing that God established with the nation of Israel, it's evident that they often had conflicted relationships with the other nations of the world. Of primary importance to God was that the Israelites not engage in the worship of the gods of the other nations around them. In a sense, this was the whole meaning of the Exodus from Egypt; through Moses, God led his people away from Egypt so that they could worship him on his terms. In Exodus 6:7, we read that the Lord said to Moses:

> I will take you to be my people, and I will be your God, and you shall know that I am the Lord your God, who has brought you out from under the burdens of the Egyptians.

Thus it was that Moses appeared before the Pharaoh on numerous occasions saying, *"Let my people go, that they may serve me,"* (Exodus 9:1).

Israel's conflict with other nations arose in a variety of contexts. One of the most notable examples concerned their conquest of the Canaanites for the possession of their land because of God's original promise to Abraham. Often, Israel's conflicts with the nations around them had to do with the distinctiveness of their worship in contrast to that of those nations. The children of Israel are frequently reminded of their unique calling to love the Lord their God will all their hearts.

> Hear, O Israel: The Lord our God, the Lord is one. You shall love the Lord your God with all your heart and with all your soul and with all your might. (Deuteronomy 6:4–5).

> When you enter the land the Lord your God is giving you, do not learn to imitate the detestable ways of the nations there ... Anyone who does these things is detestable to the Lord; because of these same detestable practices the Lord your God will drive out those nations before you. (Deuteronomy 18: 9, 12, NIV).

Through invasion from other nations and ultimately through exile from their own land, God's judgement fell upon the Israelites for being unfaithful to God and breaking their covenant with him by their worship of other gods. In 2 Chronicles 36:14–16, we read this summary of the reason for God's judgement against his own people:

> All the officers of the priest and the people like-
> wise were exceedingly unfaithful, following all
> the abominations of the nations. And they pol-
> luted the house of the Lord that he had made
> holy in Jerusalem. The Lord, the God of their
> fathers, sent persistently to them by his messen-
> gers, because he had compassion on his people
> and on his dwelling place. But they kept mocking
> the messengers of God, despising his words and
> scoffing at his prophets, until the wrath of the
> Lord rose against his people, until there was
> no remedy.

From this description of Israel's unique call to worship and subsequent unfaithfulness, there are a couple of noteworthy observations: one, Israel's call to the worship of God as the one true God of the whole universe; and two, this brought them into conflict with nations that were polytheistic and animistic in their worship practices. Even though the Israelites were often unfaith-ful to their calling, what set them apart from their neighbours was their rejection of pluralism. This constantly placed them in a posi-tion of tension with those other nations. It raised the question of how faithful Israelites should try to live their lives in this situation. In a very real way, it is not unlike the challenge Christians face in seeking to live out their faith in these postmodern times so characterized by religious pluralism.

Like the Israelites, and based upon God's revelation in the scriptures to them, Christians, by the uniqueness of their faith, also feel called to the worship of the one true God. This sets them apart from the religious practices of most other peoples of the world. At the same time, they want to do whatever they can to live peaceably with people who have differing religious practices—partially, of course, for their own benefit.

There is another dimension to this relationship: the desire to "tell the truth" about God's call to true worship through faith in Jesus Christ so that others might turn from their pagan practices to worship God acceptably. Having come to experience worship in the way that God has revealed it (and despite their own short-comings), they are motivated by a true sense of compassion to spread the good news concerning the kingdom of Jesus Christ, inviting as many as possible to become participants.

Of course, to the average postmodern person of our times, this sounds like a whole lot of religious superiority and bigotry. After all, a major tenet of postmodern thought is that any claim to an all-encompassing metanarrative that seeks to explain the reason for human existence in an exclusive way is rather ludicrous as well as offensive. Yet the whole point of the Christian gospel is that such a metanarrative indeed exists. This conviction and commitment is largely based on what has always been considered reasonable historical and internal evidence for the validity of the Bible. But this potential conflict does raise the question of how Christians might authentically live and communicate their faith in this environment.

The Bible itself contains many examples of faithful individuals and people who attempted to live out their true faith in God amidst people who worshipped and lived in ways that were contrary to

God's self-revelation. How God's people practiced their faith in relation to their neighbours is a major theme throughout the Jewish and Christian scriptures.

A striking example is the prophet Jonah, whom God called to preach to Israel's enemy, the Assyrian Ninevites. The story of Jonah is a sad commentary on Jonah's initial resistance to go to these people, but the story demonstrates God's great compassion for people beyond Israel's borders. The New Testament is also filled with stories of Jesus and his followers reaching out to people outside of Israel with the good news of God's love and forgiveness, because as the angel said to the shepherds at the time of Jesus' birth, *"Fear not, for behold, I bring you good news of great joy that will be for all the people,"* (Luke 2:10). Jesus himself said, *"... this gospel of the kingdom will be proclaimed throughout the whole world as a testimony to all nations, and then the end will come,"* (Matthew 24:14). One of the great challenges facing the Christian church throughout its history has been how to effectively communicate God's good news concerning Jesus to a world that is often disinterested and even hostile towards those who identify with it or seek to share it with others.

One of my favourite examples of a person who seemed especially gifted in knowing how to live and communicate God's wisdom in a hostile environment is the prophet Daniel. I think the story of Daniel offers some excellent insights into what it means for Christians to live out their faith in the postmodern world. The story is set in the time of Israel's exile from the land of Israel to Babylon when King Nebuchadnezzar successfully invaded Jerusalem in 605 B.C. At that time, Daniel, along with several other young men of noble birth, were chosen to be educated in the language and culture of the Chaldeans, with a view to ultimate service in the foreign king's court. It was in that context that Daniel and his friends encountered some huge challenges to their faith while they also tried to understand their new culture and relate to it in a way that was positive and productive.

It's important to note that the situation in which Daniel found himself was not of his own doing; it was something orchestrated by the sovereign will of God amid Israel's unfaithfulness. Similarly, we may find ourselves in circumstances over which we have no direct control. Yet in God's sovereign doings, he allows situations to emerge that call faithful people to experience special outpourings of God's wisdom. Thankfully, as is evident in this story, God can bring good out of happenings that may otherwise seem very difficult.

King Nebuchadnezzar obviously was no fool when it came to recognize the good resources from Israel that could benefit his kingdom. Among those he had taken captive, he was looking for qualities that defined royalty in his day. In many ways, through our programs of athletics and education, our governments and educators still look for these same qualities today—physical attractiveness and fitness (athleticism), an aptitude for knowledge and skill, the ability to relate to the culture of the day, and the qualifications to serve as leaders in business, education, law, medicine, architecture, engineering, government and so on. Much like educational programs of our times, Nebuchadnezzar's plan was to instruct these subjects for three years before placing them in his service. In fact, his plan was so intentional that it appears to have been a residence program that also included a dietary regimen which he himself established.

Nebuchadnezzar also arranged a name change for each of his understudies. He actually took their Hebrew names, all of which referred to the God of Israel in some way, and changed them to reflect the religion of the Babylonians. Variously interpreted, their names were changed in the following ways: Daniel (*God is my judge*) became Belteshazzar (*may Bel protect his life*); Hannaniah (*God is gracious*) became Shadrack (*the command of the Sumurian moon god, Aku*); Mishael (*Who is what God is?*) was changed to Mischach (*Who is what Aku is?*); and Azariah (*God has helped*) became Abednego (*servant of Nebo*). Since naming is universally significant as a way of pointing to one's lifelong identity, often also with religious meaning, these name-changes must have represented a difficult transition for these men.

Obviously, they couldn't do much about the pagan names assigned to them, but that didn't mean they couldn't maintain their Hebrew identity otherwise. One of the ways in which Daniel and his three friends decided to preserve their cultural distinctiveness was to maintain a diet, likely more in line with their Hebrew heritage. Their strategy was to demonstrate to the king that they had distinctive cultural practices that could serve his ultimate interests. At the same time, by God's help, they were also able to prove their educational proficiency regarding the Chaldean culture. In the end, the king "...*found them ten times better than all the magicians and enchanters that were in all his kingdom*" (Daniel 1:20).

One of the outstanding features of this story is how Daniel and his friends maintained their Jewish faith while also appreciating features of the foreign culture into which their lives were thrust. Those who know this story also know that God gave Daniel and his friends special favour and government appointment in this foreign culture because of what turned out to be Daniel's supernatural ability to interpret the king's dream.

Daniel and his friends lived with a great deal of potential risk to their lives, but they knew when and how to resist the kind of cultural engagement that would ultimately compromise their God-given convictions. The third chapter of Daniel is especially poignant in this regard, as it describes what happened when Daniel's three friends refused to serve the gods of Babylon or worship the image (the head of gold, representative of King Nebuchadnezzar himself). Their punishment for this refusal was to be thrown into a very hot furnace.

Though we know of their amazing miraculous survival in this ordeal, it's important to recognize that they were prepared for the ultimate sentence of death in these circumstances. Yet they were resolute before the king, *"... that we will not serve your gods or worship the golden image that you have set up,"* (Daniel 3:18). In the end, by their unwillingness to yield to the pressure of pluralism, they were honoured not only by their God in his unusual protection of them, but also by the king himself, who commended them as those *"... who trusted in Him, and set aside the king's command, and yielded up their bodies rather than serve and worship any god except their own God,"* (Daniel 3:28). Because of their actions, the king also took a couple other notable measures: he decreed that if anyone spoke against the God of these men, they would be killed. Additionally, he promoted the three to new positions of responsibility and honour in his government.

We could go on to look at another example from the life of Daniel concerning his refusal to yield to the large degree of political pressure from his peers when, because of jealousy, they tried to trap him into not giving exclusive (religious) allegiance to the Median King Darius. Once again, God intervened on Daniel's behalf, protecting him from certain death when thrown into a den of lions, but also vindicating him before the king and his peers regarding the truth of his religion (Daniel 6).

Daniel's example offers today's Christians a great deal of wisdom about how to conduct their lives in a culture that has become increasingly separated from its Christian foundations (to the extent that such existed in the first place). Like the early Christians in the time of Caesar-worship in the Roman Empire, there are times when those identified as true believers face the challenge of distinguishing between a proper sense of allegiance to a secular or pagan government (Romans 13:1–2; Titus 3:1), and maintaining a strong sense of commitment to the One who has made himself known in the Bible and in his son, Jesus Christ.

Jesus himself was challenged to make this distinction when those who were plotting against him tried to trap him regarding his allegiance to Caesar: "*Is it lawful to pay taxes to Caesar?*" (Matthew 22:17). Jesus' brilliant answer was to ask for a coin that had Caesar's image on it. His conclusion was that God and Caesar represented two different worlds, both requiring separate kinds of allegiance. Caesar was merely a human ruler that God had appointed to govern in the affairs of humanity for a limited time. Only God in heaven was deserving of worship, because he was the ultimate authority. Jesus made this same distinction in his ignominious trial before the Jewish high priest (John 18:19–24) as well as to Pilate, the Roman governor. To the latter he said, "*You would have no authority over me at all unless it had been given you from above,*" (John 19:11).

These examples illustrate the delicate balance to which Christians today are called to live in relation to God and their post-modern culture. Like Daniel, they need to respect the culture in which they live, seeking to understand and learn from it to make the best possible contribution. On the other hand, when circum-stances or governmental decisions require them to compromise on legitimate expressions of true worship, they will necessarily have to choose ways that can only be regarded as being counterculture.

Daniel's example leads us to the conclusion that Christians are called to live prophetically. That simply means that Christians need to live, speak, and serve in a way that wisely witnesses to the truth of God's self-revelation in the natural world, in the Bible, and in Jesus Christ. As those who are identified as the *"salt of the earth"* (Matthew 5:13), Christians can only have that salutary effect upon the mainstream of human society if they retain a distinctively biblical commitment.

One possible response for Christians in the face of ridicule of one kind or another is to react with similar words of disrespect and malice. There are instances in which Christians become angry and unkind towards those who unjustly accuse them of being discriminatory and factious. That kind of response will not serve God's ultimate interest well in making the Good News known to the world. Christians need to think and pray long and hard about how to answer their critics before they do. They need to remember the proverb that says, *"A soft answer turns away wrath, but a harsh word stirs up anger,"* (Proverbs 15:1).

Another sad response often characteristic of Christians in the face of challenges from a pluralistic culture is to accommodate themselves to the point of compromise on fundamental questions of worship and appropriate behaviour. When the pressure is on to accept moral behaviours that are clearly opposed to God's way, it's easy to begin to look for answers through a re-interpretation of the sacred text, somehow concluding that new times call for new understandings of old laws. The thinking might easily be that perhaps we've misunderstood God's will concerning his abhorrence of practices such as abortion, euthanasia, and homosexuality, to name some of the more prominent current issues. Though the culture at large might approve of behaviours we believe God abhors, we need to find ways to graciously resist these practices where we can and where they affect our own lives.

Another possible reaction of Christians who are being bullied to agree with pluralism or practices that are contrary to God's truth is to withdraw from active engagement with culture for religious reasons. It seems that one of the current reactions to the changes brought on by the development of postmodernism has been for Christians to become somewhat reclusive. To use an Old Testament analogy, they tend to feel overwhelmed by the Goliath who daily stalks the land while he calls for someone to rise to the challenge of a fight. Christians often appear to be intimidated by the strong opposition that has evidently risen against their faith and the church. They lack clarity about the philosophical reasons for the opposition, and they lack spiritual and intellectual confidence about how to effectively counter the world's morally destructive tendencies.

In the face of this conflict with the postmodern world, there is a need among evangelical Christians today, like Daniel and David of a former time, for a renewed sense of courage and boldness bolstered by the kind of faith we see in these examples. It's important to remember that Daniel's courage before the idol-worshipping Nebuchadnezzar was not of his own making. Besides the sovereign God's work in his own life, Daniel's faith was based on the firm foundation of God's revelation to his people through the Law of Moses and the holy chronicles of God's dealings with his people. Daniel had a deep sense of confidence that the faith of his Jewish forefathers was much more than just another religion whose so-called deities rivaled anything close to the God he knew. In other words, even while living in a pagan culture, he understood the exquisitely unique nature of the God he served. It was the same for David in relation to the Philistines among whom he lived in his time.

With these examples in mind, it seems to me that for Christians of our times to be effective in living and communicating God's revelation in Christ, they need a renewed sense of commitment and confidence concerning the truth of the biblical account. Courage and boldness come from a deep sense of assurance that the Christian faith is not just one among many others, but that it is unique in its historical development and accuracy, as well as in the sublime virtues of which it speaks and how these may be attained. An essential element in this renewed confidence is that the Bible is trustworthy, not simply because of its reputation, but because of inherent evidence of its full and complete verbal inspiration. Without a commitment to the idea that the Bible of today is the same as the one that was textually inspired by God to human writers so many years ago, confusion about texts and their interpretation will prevail, and confidence in the uniqueness of the Christian faith will quickly fade—especially in the face of the confusion experienced in these postmodern times.

Along with such confidence in the accurate testimony of scripture, postmodern times call for a renewed commitment to the definition and nature of the gospel, since it is the power of that gospel that is effective in enabling all who believe to experience God's salvation (Romans 1:16). That conviction of truth of the good news from God must extend to the point that, consistent with what the apostles believed, it is regarded as the *only* means by which anyone can be saved (Acts 4:12). It is true that the gospel is the whole story of Jesus, which climaxes in his death and resurrection for the forgiveness of sin, as well as the impartation of his righteous and eternal life to anyone who truly believes (Titus 3:3–7). It is this gospel that is the spearhead of an effective attack on the vain human philosophies of the world in which we live.

If this kind of language makes it sound like we are engaged in a battle of sorts, then this is also consistent with the language of the Bible, where we read about Israel's conflict with its neighbours because of God's condemnation of religious idolatry (Joshua), and where we read about the reality of Christian warfare as a battle with *"spiritual forces of evil in heavenly places,"* (Ephesians 6:12). The nature of our battle today is not one of physical engagement, but rather of the kind that is able to *"... destroy arguments and every lofty opinion raised against the knowledge of God ..."* (2 Corinthians 10:5).

Such a battle requires a great deal of courage and boldness, but it also calls for an unusual sense of wisdom, as Daniel's example illustrates so well. He understood that being a noble man in a foreign culture entailed the need to respect the powers that be, not only because he didn't want to unnecessarily jeopardize his own security, but also because such respect signaled a legitimate recognition of God's sovereignty and the God-given dignity of others. It was a case of careful discernment between that which was acceptable and that which needed to be challenged. Daniel and his three friends made nothing out of their name changes and even their education (which was probably very good in many ways), but they did challenge the king's dietary regimen, which evidently was in serious conflict with their Hebrew beliefs and practices. Yet even in this, their challenge was not a direct refusal to participate but proposed in the context of "a ten-day test" (Daniel 1:12).

In the matter of bowing in worship to the golden statue (Daniel 3), Daniel's three friends knew this practice conflicted with the first and most basic law of their Hebrew faith in which it was stated that, *"You shall have no other gods before me. You shall not make for yourself a carved image... You shall not bow down to them or serve them..."* (Deuteronomy 5:7–9). Even facing the prospect of almost certain death, they were willing to refuse such a compromise. In the end, God provided miraculous protection and rescue for them. It was the same for Daniel when he was thrown into the lions' den. These stories support the principle of faith-based Christian resistance in circumstances that call for disobedience to one of God's very specific commands, but it's interesting to note that apart from those circumstances, Daniel and his friends participated fully in the foreign society of the Chaldeans.

Christians living in today's world of religious pluralism are like foreigners in a strange land. They need to be confident of their identity, which is rooted in God's revelation to the Jewish people and culminates in the coming of Jesus Christ and the establishment of his church and kingdom. While living humbly in response to God's great grace in their lives, they also need to be willing to live boldly in their God-given identity and purpose. There is no reason why they cannot or shouldn't participate fully in the world, despite their religious differences, by caring for others and supporting God's established government wherever possible. But they need to be discerning about when to take a stand against policies or pronouncements that call for them to compromise on basic spiritual loyalties. Sometimes the most effective witness to God's revelation in a religiously pluralistic society is simply that of a positive and affirming presence. In today's postmodern world, Christians should seek to be leaders in demonstrating Christian virtue in every noble endeavor through genuine care for people without discrimination. But they should also be prepared to provide a good defense, or *apologia*, for the Christian faith when required -- for the sake of effective evangelism in an otherwise religiously confused world. In short, they should be prepared to live *prophetically*.

The fact that Daniel is found in the prophetic section of the Old Testament speaks to this major aspect of his life and the times in which he lived—when government was largely directed by the advisement of magicians and spiritual prognosticators. It's not surprising that God demonstrated his power in Daniel's life through dreams and visons of various kinds. Daniel was repeatedly given insight and wisdom for the times in which he lived in a way that was superior to that of his contemporaries, often proving to be helpful and relevant to the governments and rulers of his day. Sometimes, as in the case of Nebuchadnezzar's second dream (chapter 4), and the interpretation of handwriting on the wall for Belshazzar (chapter 5), Daniel's interpretations resulted in a serious judgement toward the king. Nevertheless, in the end Daniel was recognized for his unusual insight into God's larger plans and purposes. Daniel's prominence in the Christian church today is due to his influential prophetic role in those times, but also to the fact that the largest part of his prophecies concerns the coming of Jesus Christ (Daniel 9), and God's final judgement at the end of time (Daniel 10–12).

I view Daniel as an iconic figure for Christians, illustrating how we are called to live in the world, especially during these post-modern times. It is true that most of us will never be called to the prominence of someone like Daniel; nevertheless, all Christians, by their identity and allegiance to Jesus Christ, are called to live in a way that distinguishes them as prophetic witnesses to the truth of God and his gospel. To do so, they must remember their roots in God's revelation to the Jewish people and its fulfillment in the coming of Christ. With this distinction firmly in mind, they must be willing to engage fully with their world for the sake of God's honour and the communication of the gospel. They should be prepared to defend truth about God within a pluralistic society, or when they are expected to deny some basic conviction of faith. They should be prepared to live prophetically in the sense that they witness to the continuing truth of the gospel and sometimes receive supernatural wisdom in addressing issues or needs of our day.

To live prophetically means to understand one's identity as "the salt of the earth," which Jesus mentioned in the Sermon on the Mount (Matthew 5:13). By using that analogy, Jesus instructed his followers to live in a genuinely Spirit-filled manner whereby they would be led by the Holy Spirit in every cultural engagement, seeking to consistently apply God's truth to the situations in which they found themselves. Living by the truth in their own lives and applying it to their relationships and work, God's intention is that they would have a savoury, life-preserving, and enriching effect upon their immediate culture. With a continual consciousness of God's presence and guidance, living as the salt of the earth would mean living prayerfully while sometimes privately or publicly experiencing God's supernatural intervention as a personal and open witness to his reality and the truth of his words.

We know there is an element in prophecy that is commonly recognized as predictive, but in the history of the biblical prophets, that element is relatively minor in comparison to what we might call prophecy's prescriptive element. By prescriptive we mean that God had a certain message for individuals or peoples at a specific place and point in time. As we study the major and minor prophets, we see that their prophecies contained words of judgement for their times because of God's displeasure with his people's departure from true faith. Thus, the prophets' role couldn't help but place them in a certain position of tension and even conflict, which often resulted in their persecution and death. There were other times when the prophets spoke as messengers of hope and encouragement, as in the case of Isaiah's famous comfort speeches in Isaiah 9 and 40. Despite the difficulties associated with their work, more often than not, prophets were held in high regard, because they were recognized for their godly lives and communications from God.

In the history of the church, various individuals have been willing to live out their Christian faith prophetically in relationship to the society around them. Consider the case of John Wycliffe of the fourteenth century, who by his insight and appreciation for scripture spoke out against the clerical luxuries and abuses of the church in his day, in the process becoming a powerful influence towards the Reformation of the sixteenth century. For a more recent example, consider William Wilberforce, whose evangelical Christian convictions in the late eighteenth century led him to fight for causes in the British parliament that were consistent with principles of biblical social justice, such as the abolition of the slave trade.

Even in these times we see Christian men and women who have been successful in speaking charitably, knowledgably, and wisely in a wide variety of fields challenging commonly-held notions of moral and ethical indecency as defined by the Christian scriptures. Some causes, such as human trafficking (i.e. specifically the trading of children and youth for sexual slavery of one kind or another), are those in which Christians often lead and receive widespread support from the public and governments who legislate accordingly. Yet there are many other causes of a moral nature, such as fetal abortions, euthanasia, or homosexuality, that make it more difficult for Christians to speak out simply because of disagreement, even sometimes among themselves, about what is biblically taught. In the end, as followers of Jesus, Christians have a responsibility to prophetically challenge notions that are not in keeping with the clear directives of scripture.

One other element in prophetic service consists of the experience and demonstration of the miraculous. It is evident in the Daniel example that God intervened in supernatural ways to authenticate the unique and powerful Jewish faith of Daniel and his friends. In answer to prayer, God provided accurate interpretations of dreams, protected them in the flames, shut the lions' mouths, and fulfilled prophetic (predictive) messages.

It is also interesting to note the prominence of prayer in relationship to the supernatural experiences of Daniel and his three friends. In Daniel, we see prayer used as a request for God's intervention (Daniel 2), as worship and discipline (chapter 6), and as deep confession of sin (chapter 9). We conclude from these examples that for Christians of any time to live as "the salt of the earth," they need to be the kind of people whose unique faith is authenticated by obvious interventions of God's presence and power. Without a doubt, a key factor in this experience is their willingness to engage in various expressions of prayer.

Historically, this element of the miraculous has played a significant role in the progress of the gospel around the world. What largely characterized the church from its beginning, as is evident in the book of Acts, has continued to be a major factor in the expansion of God's kingdom and the building of his church. There are many examples of major demonstrations of God's power over the effects of sin, such as disease and demonic activity, especially on the frontiers of Christian mission expansion.

In its relatively short history of about 130 years, the denomination in which I have served (the Christian and Missionary Alliance) has continuously emphasized the importance of prayer and the miraculous power of the Holy Spirit. Founder, Albert Simpson, spoke often of "Jesus as healer," insisting biblically that Jesus' atoning sacrifice for sin and his astounding resurrection also included provision for physical healing as demonstrated by Jesus' own healing ministry. There is no doubt that the practice of prayer for healing in the Alliance, and the resulting instances of God's miraculous intervention, have been major factors in its growth and development around the world. I have seen instances of miraculous healing in my own pastoral experience. At the same time, it's important to provide biblical teaching that explains the value of suffering and why it is that sometimes God, due to his sovereign will and purpose, doesn't answer our prayers for healing or for changes to our circumstances.

Miracles have also been a major emphasis in what became known as the "signs and wonders movement" of the 1980s and 90s. John Wimber, a prominent leader within the movement that eventually give birth to the Association of Vineyard Churches, believed that the communication of the gospel could proceed more effectively if there were supernatural signs and wonders at the same time. Though it's important to exercise discernment, because of the possibility of counterfeit spiritualties and powers as well as emotional appealing excesses, it's hard to resist the truth behind obvious examples of God's supernatural work in people's lives.

In summary, the church in these postmodern times stands in a precarious place. On the one hand, it is easily vulnerable to an undiscerning sense of accommodation or reclusiveness regarding current cultural trends. On the other hand, the church is confronted with the challenge of living prophetically in the same spirit and wisdom that characterized the prophet Daniel. A pertinent question is whether the church of these times will become accommodating and reclusive, or rise to the challenge of a compassionate and wise defence of the Christian faith for the sake of the gospel and its mission.

CHAPTER 9

Essential Elements in Postmodern Church Ministry

To illustrate something of the changes in church ministry that have taken place over the last four or five decades, here is a bit of an overview of my own pastoral ministry journey. I was still in seminary when I entered pastoral church ministry in Saskatchewan in 1971. I was thrilled by the opportunity to serve in the role of Assistant Pastor of a major denominational church. In my enthusiasm to serve, I had no idea about the complexity that church ministry entailed, but it seems to me, in retrospect, that it was not nearly as challenging as it has become in recent times.

Thankfully, due to good theological instruction at the time and some helpful mentoring, I was able to acquire a basic knowledge of the skills needed for effective pastoral work. As an assistant pastor, my responsibilities focused on the oversight and development of the youth ministry, with special responsibility for high school young people. Through an earlier Christian student ministry influence, the Navigators, I had learned the value of various spiritual disciplines including means of Bible study, prayer, and evangelism, that became valuable as tools for this ministry.

I also had the opportunity to participate in the work of the church's Christian education committee, whose responsibility it was to provide Bible education for children, youth, and adults in the life of the church. A volunteer leader on the committee (who was also a good friend and on staff at our nearby seminary) and I worked together at developing our own adult Sunday School curriculum. We used a simple method dubbed, "hook, book, look, took," based on the work of a prominent Bible education leader at the time, Larry Richards. It turned out to be an effective way to help Christian adults study the Bible with a view to its application in their own lives.

Beyond these major responsibilities that first year, I was also coached in the fine art of pastoral care. Besides being on hand for personal crisis intervention ministries, I discovered that pastoral care involved meeting people in their homes for more personal kinds of ministry. I learned that the most effective way to do individual pastoral care was to listen and ask good questions, which potentially could lead to issues of personal faith and biblically-based solutions.

But by far the biggest challenge of all in that first year was the occasional responsibility to preach in a Sunday worship service. At that stage of my pastoral ministry development, I could easily identify with Moses, who remonstrated in his response to God's call, saying, "... *I am not eloquent* ... *I am slow of speech and of tongue*," (Exodus 4:10). I also learned that preaching, in contrast to more personal ministries, was an amazing way for God to sovereignly speak to people in ways that were often completely unknown to the speaker.

Though I still had much to learn about pastoral ministry in those "modern times," it wasn't long before my wife and I moved on to my own pastoral charge in a smaller Saskatchewan community. We

arrived as a young couple, eager and optimistic to make a difference in the life of a church that was struggling with a bit of spiritual
illness due to some degree of internal division. With our arrival
and by God's grace, it was evident that a fresh breeze of hope
began blowing bringing new signs of life into that congregation.

As a young pastor, my focus was on trying to prepare and
preach two different messages each Sunday (one for the morning
and another for the evening), to plan for a Wednesday evening
prayer meeting, and to lead a Friday evening youth meeting. In
between, because there was no other help, I spent my time answer-
ing the phone, visiting with people who came to the office, and
publishing a weekly church bulletin on the church's mimeograph
machine. Besides preparing for the monthly board meetings, I also
tried to do a certain number of weekly home visits. It's exhausting
just to think about it now and to consider all that was involved in
trying to pastor a small church in those times.

One of the characteristics of those modern times (something
more obvious now in hind-sight), was that the business of the
church and ministry seemed to take precedence over everything
else, including the development of one's family life. Though
our four children were born to us during our eight-year span of
service in that community I spent a lot of time in church ministry.
By contrast, and quite commendably I believe, today's postmodern
culture leads young pastors to have more time for relaxation and the
development of family relationships. This may also be the reason
they often arrange for occasional extended rest-and-study leaves,
called sabbaticals – something not nearly as common in modern
times. Possibly these less-stringent practices are partially explained
by the greater emphasis now on one's emotional wellbeing.

Besides everything else, there were special pastoral responsibilities involving weddings, funerals, and some counselling. In

these circumstances, figuring out how to put together a weekly schedule proved to be the biggest challenge of all. Evangelism happened through personal contacts and somewhat also through the Sunday worship services. About every six weeks or so, the local radio station did a live broadcast of our Sunday morning service, something quite unusual these days.

Thankfully, after having a couple of excellent consecutive pastoral interns from our College and Seminary, the church hired one of them as an assistant pastor. Soon the church grew, not only because of the new energy and ideas that came by way of additional help, but also because of a greater sense of vision to make a larger Christian impact on the community.

Much of the latter was inspired by the church growth philosophy of the time, and by international Christian leaders who had experience and big ideas about effectively reaching out to larger numbers of people. It wasn't too long before the church in this smaller community committed to sell its small residential-street building and sacrificially invest in the construction of a much larger facility on a main thoroughfare surrounding the city.

At that time, church development was all about the visibility and accessibility of the building. Christian ministry expansion was mostly about programs that took place at the building site. In that late modern era, effective church ministry had a lot to do with the prominence of the building.

After a time, with that same philosophy in mind, we sensed God's call to a church ministry in a much larger Saskatchewan community. There the challenge for effective growth and development was considerably more complex. Already a slight cultural shift towards new ways of thinking about life and church ministry was beginning to emerge. This was the time, for example, when Sunday evening services gave way to more individual family time, and the mid-week church prayer meeting (as well as the pre-worship service Sunday School) yielded to the development of a variety of mid-week home Bible study group meetings. Church services also began to reflect a bit more informality, moving away from formal hymn-book singing to worship choruses using an "overhead projector."

In the early days of my pastoral ministry, and consistent with the structuralism of the modern era, at least in my experience, it seemed that churches followed more of a corporate model of organization. But by the late 80s and 90s, it was evident that there was a growing sense of resistance towards thinking of church as a building, a business, or an institution. Though we weren't aware of that shift at the time, now in retrospect, it's possible to see a trend in the mainstream culture that was also beginning to affect the local church.

When, a few years later, we moved on to pastoral ministry in a major center in British Columbia, over the span of almost twenty years of service there, it was evident that this trend continued to increase. At first, as in Saskatchewan, the church in BC continued with many programs in the building, including a pre-service Sunday School, a Sunday evening service, and a mid-week prayer meeting. But over time, with the help and approval of lay church leaders and consistent with trends in other churches, changes were introduced that seemed to be more in keeping with the less formal tendencies in the surrounding culture.

Much to the disappointment of my "modern" way of thinking, despite the physical growth of the congregation and the large opportunity in the surrounding community, this British Columbia church consistently declined the idea of facility expansion or relocation. Instead, it opted to support the idea of minor physical improvements to the existing building and an additional church development in the city. Influenced by new ways of thinking about how to expand church ministry, knowledgeable and enterprising members of a home group in the church felt that they wanted to take on the challenge of starting an additional church in our city. Their interest, it was evident, was for a church that was less formal and more inviting to people who were unfamiliar with church, or for any number of reasons, had become disconnected with the church.

Consequently, instead of expanding our own facilities or beginning plans toward a church relocation program of our own, our church, through its Elders Board, opted to arrange for the planting of a new church. We engaged the members of the home group with these interests, to set up a steering committee by which to sketch a plan and to find an appropriate pastor. In the end, working together, we found a pastor who had special abilities and vision for reaching out to people he dubbed "PMs" ("postmoderns"). With the help of the denomination, the prospective pastor moved his family to our city and began to engage in an intentional process of praying, planning, and strategizing with our church ("the mother church") and with those interested in starting a "daughter church." The group secured a rented facility for their initial meetings and, at a Worship Service in the spring of 1997 at the "mother church," ten families were commissioned for this new venture.

It is interesting to note that even up to the present time, consistent with postmodern cultural trends, the stated philosophy of the "daughter" church has been decidedly different from what had been standard fare among most evangelical churches of the time. The pastor, who had special talents for graphic arts, blitzed an area of the city with an attractive brochure that outlined the nature of the new church. Its appeal was especially to those who were looking for something more culturally relevant in church life and ministry. The brochure said it would be "a church for the changing times."

Based on a semi-formal community survey conducted by the pastor and church lay leaders the brochure said that Sunday services would be a maximum of one hour in length and would consist of music much like the kind people listened to everyday on commercial radio. Furthermore, it said, attendees could "come as they are" as far as their dress was concerned, and that there would be no mention of money or finances (something the members of the new church considered offensive to non-church people).

Needless to say, the promotional piece got a good deal of attention both in the community and among other churches, because it challenged many existing church ministry traditions. Over time, the new church plant attracted a relatively large number of people who were looking for a church as advertised. Many, who otherwise would likely have continued their lives apart from church, came to see what this new church was all about and eventually became baptized Christians and full participants in the life of the church. Although since then the church has become more conventional in many ways, it still carries features that reflect postmodern trends. For example, in line with its anti-institutional leanings, after twenty years of existence, it has a down-town office, but quite intentionally continues to use rented facilities for its Sunday services -- in a building normally used for live theatre.

During most of my years of resident pastoral ministry, even though I saw numerous changes in church ministry practice, I had never stopped to consider the reason for these changes from a philosophical or sociological point of view. My practice generally was to prayerfully ponder what other churches were doing to be more relevant, reflect some on those practices theologically and biblically, and then attempt to lead the church toward the application of some of those same practices. In many cases, of course, these changes did not come about without some measure of pain, tension, and loss. But through further study and research since then, as well as experience, I think I've gained a better grasp on some of the reasons for the radical changes that have occurred. Based on a better understanding of biblical history, philosophy, and theology, I think I've also been able to assess how some of these changes have been beneficial and, in other cases, how they may also been counter-productive.

For the past eleven years or so, I have been actively involved in transitional pastoral ministry, mostly with churches of my own denomination. Ironically, the role itself developed out of new ideas about how my denomination such as mine traditionally processed pastoral changes for churches. When I began in this kind of work, and for years before that time, most pastoral changes in our denomination were arranged by a regional leader called the District Superintendent. Perhaps influenced by business models, most pastors prepared to move to a new location, usually after a period of about five years or less. Though they often spoke of relocation plans in terms of God's leading (sometimes quite euphemistically, no doubt), their decision was often based on practical considerations. It's apparent that a pastor's decision to move on was often prompted by the invitation of the denominational leader for a new opportunity of service. In some cases, the move to a new location may have been due to the emergence of some congregational difficulty or various family considerations. Or often the progressive work of an aspiring pastor in one location was deemed to be beneficial in another center. In those times it seems, pastoral service in our denomination was usually characterized by rather short periods of service and frequent moves.

In that time, district superintendents appeared to have a significant degree of authority to make relocation recommendations to pastors and churches without a great deal of resistance from either.

But in the 80s and 90s, a new generation of pastors increasingly resisted the idea of having to move often, partially for personal reasons concerning family and financial stability, but partly also because they wanted to genuinely invest in a church and community for longer-term change. This adjustment, I suspect, flowed out of an unconscious desire to be more authentic about pastoral ministry in that way. Whereas a former generation thought more in terms of numerical growth success, a new generation of pastors could more easily be satisfied with smaller signs of progress.

Certainly, this had begun to be the pattern in my own experience. Though numerical growth did occur through various means of evangelism, even when growth was slow, my inclination was to continue working with a congregation for long-term results. In a couple of cases, I continued for much longer periods of service than those churches had previously experienced. I was also interested in how these churches overtime could gain a higher profile and have a greater impact in a community. I realize now that this change in approach to pastoral longevity seemed to have a lot to do with the cultural shift that was also occurring at the same time.

About the time that resident pastoral ministry ended for me, a significant change had taken place in how pastors and churches navigated the matter of pastoral change. Due to a variety of reasons, the whole matter of pastoral relocation became increasingly complex. For one thing, as I mentioned earlier, the regional denominational leader no longer seemed to exercise as much initiative to affect pastoral change for churches. Additionally, it appeared, congregations seemed to want much more control in who they called to be their church pastors. Also, pastors as well as churches were finding it more difficult to come to conclusions about how and why pastors should move to a new location. Sometimes pastors tended to wait too long before making a move. As differences about effective ministry due to cultural changes grew, churches often took more liberty in applying upward pressure on their pastors to move. Predictably, this kind of tension frequently resulted in rather unhealthy departures.

Because I experienced a little of this pattern in my own pastoral ministry, I decided to write my doctoral dissertation on the reason for unhealthy pastoral transitions in my own denomination. Based on the qualitative analysis of this study, it became evident that in at least fifty per cent of the cases, pastoral transitions were accompanied by a good deal of acrimony—both for churches and for pastors. A similar study I conducted for our denomination in our provincial region came to the same conclusion. Thankfully, the denomination recognized this unhealthy pattern and determined to take more care in helping pastors and churches prepare for better transitions.

Part of this care involved helping churches do a better job of preparing for their next pastor. In recent years, many denominations have seen the wisdom of encouraging churches to contract a pastoral transition specialist who can help the church prepare for a healthy pastoral search. Much of this development has also been due to the work of a Christian ministry called, Outreach Canada. Among other kinds of analysis for churches, this organization works at developing tools and training for pastors to assist churches through times of crisis and transition. It has been a very helpful resource in the development of my own work with churches in transition.

Typically, a transition pastor will serve, as a resident pastor for the church in a transition period for as little as six, and sometimes up to eighteen months. The average time for me in a dozen churches over the last eleven years has been about nine months. Right from the beginning, the transition pastor will make it clear to the lay leadership Board and the church congregation that he is not a candidate for the job. The focus is on helping the church affect a good sense of closure on the past, ensuring the provision of effective pastoral services in the interim, while also working with the Board and the church towards preparation for a good pastoral search process. The transition pastor will ensure that there is good communication and organization throughout the church while also seeing that people are properly cared for (shepherded) during his time of service.

Often the transition pastor's responsibilities will involve working with existing staff by helping them refine their roles and assess their performance. Though there are different models of transition pastoral ministry, frequently the transition pastor will also provide the sermon for the regular Sunday services of the church, thereby communicating with the church about the essentials of transition and what the church's biblical calling and ministry is all about.

A large part of the transition pastor's work concerns a process of seeking to affect a systematic assessment of the church's culture and ministry, offering suggestions about how it might be improved to better fulfill a well-defined sense of vision. As a transition pastor, it is my responsibility to determine the underlying values that drive the main ministry and focus of the church. I've discovered that it is these values, often held subconsciously, that define the culture of a church. A good grasp of a church's understanding of its values can change the vision and culture of a church for good, and hopefully more in keeping with God's will. I will have more to say about this in the section in this chapter entitled, "Vision."

Sometimes it is evident that churches are still working with a modern era paradigm, not discerning some of the reasons for the changes that have taken place in the surrounding culture. As they prepare for future ministry, I believe it is helpful for such churches to be culturally aware and theologically discerning about points of congruence and difference with a view to more gospel ministry effectiveness.

In my transition work with churches my hope is that I can assist them and their leaders in appreciating some of the main features of the kind of biblically-based pastoral leadership that can help them become more effective even in these more faith-challenging times. In the following descriptions, based on my understanding and experience, I try to identify some of what I believe are the main features of productive pastoral work. Hopefully, these elements will stand the test of universal application because of their biblical foundations, but I think they are especially important considerations for Western forms of Christian life and ministry in these postmodern times.

Authenticity

I wrote earlier about the current thirst for authenticity. This quest has increased in these times due to a combination of the perceived lack of a meaningful metanarrative and its effect on the relative importance of existential experience. Often the desire for authenticity takes the form of greater personal transparency, even about failures. In some ways, it's a reaction to the tendency in the modern era to present an impression of competent control. Today it's more acceptable to acknowledge one's shortcomings, because it's understood that everyone is flawed in one way or another. After all, it's perceived, we live in a chaotic, imperfect world.

Though the human tendency is always towards creating a good impression, the inclination now towards candidness about difficulties is more consistent, in some ways, with biblical faith. In that context, after all, *"... there is none righteous, no, not one,"* (Romans 3:10, KJV)! But for someone who professes to be a follower of Jesus, and who has experienced the "new birth" of God's Spirit, it's also important to seek to be genuine about faith experience and practice. This is especially true for those who identify as Christian leaders or church pastors.

This quality, it seems, is most foundational to everything else in the service of the church. If authenticity is the ability to be genuine, to live life without any sense of pretense or façade, then this fits with the biblical concept of what it means to be sincere, as spoken of in Romans 12:9, where we are told that, *"Love must be sincere,"*[44] (NIV), or in 1 Timothy 1:5, where we read that, *"The goal of this command is love, which comes from a pure heart and a good conscience and a sincere faith,"* (NIV). Contrary to popular opinion, the origin of the word "sincere" in these passages is not clear, but at the very least we can conclude that it means "without pretense."

This basic quality for ministry involves, first and foremost, self-honesty. We might commonly think of this in terms of what it means to live with a clear conscience, of living in the light as God is in the light (1 John 1:5-7). It is living truthfully at the most basic level of existence. Authenticity recognizes one's ultimate accountability to God. But we may also speak of authenticity in our relationships with others. It concerns whether we are willing to be vulnerable and open with others in our lives.

For pastors to be effective in their pastoral ministry and in their preaching and personal ministries, they need to demonstrate that they are willing to be honest about their doubts, their emotional and

---

44 New International Version

spiritual struggles, including such matters as prayer, or the honest application of the Bible to their lives. In this way, they show that they identify with the struggles that people have in their own lives and communities. At the same time, pastors need to demonstrate that they are making progress, growing in grace and understanding, and in obedience to Christ.

Authenticity can also be strengthened in pastors' ministries through diligence in personal follow-up to individual needs. If ever there was a time that church leaders need to show that they deeply care, it's in these postmodern times. This is something that the great advance in technology can either impede or facilitate. In the former case, even social media can be a means of conducting superficial relationships or of causing one to lapse into self-absorption. On the other hand, technology can genuinely allow for wider expressions of personal transparency.

In the end, authenticity in these ways will go a long way to facilitating more effective kinds of service for the kingdom of God. Authenticity sums up well how one's basic personal character is relevant to ministry. Out of this genuineness in truth flows other character features, such as love, compassion, honesty, reliability, consistency, perseverance, and loyalty. In these times, pastors and Christian leaders will undoubtedly be much more effective if they are willing to be authentic.

Vision

From time to time in my pastoral transition experience, I've been asked my opinion on the greatest need in the churches with which I work. I think I've concluded that the greatest reason for a lack of progress in church ministry, from an organizational perspective, comes down to the lack of a clear sense of vision. This lack is most often reflected in various expressions of mediocrity in the life of the church. Congregants faithfully come to the public services, but they don't truly engage with any deep sense of enthusiasm and commitment. Participation at all levels begins to wane, including in the critical matter of finances. In this circumstance, there is little sense of how existing ministries relate to the larger purpose of the church. Ministries appear to happen without a sense of intentionality. There is, within the church and those ministries, a serious lack of passion or clear compulsion.

From my own experience, I understand how easily this happens. Vision tends to dissipate amid a myriad of routine responsibilities that seem to constantly call for attention. I think about this in the context of this writing project. It's easy to get bogged down in the details of writing and to slowly lose sight of the main purpose. As I write, I find myself constantly having to fight distraction of various kinds—phone calls, text messages, e-mails, beautiful summer weather, other practical responsibilities around home, hunger, weariness, and emotional discouragement. Yet I realize that to get the job done, I must keep the passion alive. Passion, I find, feeds on the clarity of vision. Often, I find my vision and passion rekindled by a special experience of God's grace – a new insight through Bible reading and prayer, through a conversation with a friend, perhaps through another kind of reading, or even through a song. By these means, I'm reminded of how important it is to continue doing what I'm doing. By this process, I see more clearly that the long hours and mental exertion are worth it.

"*Where there is no vision,*" the Bible says, "*the people perish,*" (Proverbs 29:18, KJV). In the words of the American Standard Version (ASV), "*the people cast off restraint.*" In other words, it's through the lack of clear vision that people defer to other interests and become distracted, often becoming lethargic and, in the context of the Christian faith, idolatrous.

When Moses met with God on Mount Sinai and was away from the people for some time, they quickly became distracted and asked Aaron to fashion a golden calf that they could worship (Exodus 32). This is a vivid illustration of what happens when people lose sight of their primary reason for existence. It also demonstrates the critical relationship between leadership and vision.

Vision is always tied to leadership. One of the most important elements in good leadership is the capacity to identify and communicate vision. I believe it's one way to think about the nature of preaching and sermon delivery. It seems to me that preaching is much more than methodical Bible teaching. Certainly, it entails a comprehensive exposition of the Bible and theology. But properly understood, preaching seeks to bring the meaning of a passage to bear on the larger purpose of the church and living as a Christian. Preaching vision, I believe, is a message for a specific group of people, in a definite geographical location, at a certain point in time. It is the voice of God's Spirit to the church, speaking in support and in application of biblical truth. In that way, it is the responsibility of the pastor to be a kind of "seer" or "prophet" for the congregation. By means of preaching, the pastor develops and promotes the vision of the church.

But what is this thing called "vision?" I like Bob Biehl's concept of vision, when he speaks of it in terms of *needs* in the community that makes one, "... feel deeply burdened about and uniquely qualified to meet."[45] His way of identifying this is to ask the ques-

---

45 Bob Biehl, *Masterplanning* (Mount Dora, FL: Aylen Publishing, 2005), 27.

tion, "What is it that makes you weep and pound the table?"[46] For a pastor, this question is answered through spending time in biblical meditation and prayer. It will undoubtedly also involve collaboration with other Christian leaders in the church. It is all about understanding something of God's heart, based on scripture, for a unique group of people. It is the development of a spiritual burden about the needs of people in a community in line with God's will as revealed in Scripture. As was true for the prophets of old time, it is seeing the spiritual condition of people from God's point of view and then seeking to speak to that need. Upon closer observation, it's evident that vision is really another name for faith. If faith is trusting God for the fulfillment of something he has revealed but isn't yet actually visible, then faith is the vision to see it accomplished.

Vision is commonly understood as a simple catch-phrase that identifies the main purpose of an organization or church. That may be fine, but most of the time the emphasis seems to be on formulating the catch-phrase rather than on truly representing the heart and soul of why a group exists. More likely, the vision of any group is reflected in the underlying (often unconscious) values of why a group exists and functions as it does. This is also true for families. Every family's culture (its ways of processing life as seen in its unique schedules, meals, humour, work ethic, vacation, etc.) is formed by certain stated or non-stated values that reflect and support a larger family vision. It is the underlying values that define the culture of any family, church, or organization. But it all starts with the identification and communication of a basic understanding of where life is going -- something which we call, vision. This is first and foremost the responsibility of the leader, or, in the

46 Ibid., 28.

case of the church, the pastor. In the case of the family, obviously, it would be the parents. (Much more could be written about developing values and vision in family life.)

In my work as a transition pastor, I've seen that it is helpful for a church to try to identify its primary values through an assessment process. Often this is done through a congregational survey about why people came to a particular church and what has kept them there. Sometimes this understanding of values will come through experienced observation. In this way, it is possible to describe the culture of the church—that is, the specific way and reason a church functions as it does. Some of those values may be positive, but some of them may exist in opposition to the main purpose of a church. Good values need to be strengthened, and negative ones need to be identified and abandoned. To reiterate, it is the responsibility of the pastor to speak to the development of values that are in keeping with the biblical revelation. In this process, the pastor can clarify and develop the best possible vision of that church for its ministry in the community. If it can be encapsulated in a short statement, so much the better, but the main thing is that the congregation shares a clear and deep understanding of the reason for its existence. As it is continually held before the people's hearts and minds through the Sunday sermons and in a myriad of other ways, it's possible for that vision to become an unconscious reality so that it eventually defines the very culture or ethos of the church. Vision is often something more "felt than telt." It is something evident in the atmosphere of the entire church community because of the values nurtured by the leaders.

If vision can be clarified through this kind of process, I believe it will make a huge difference in the ability of a church to accomplish God's mission in a community. In all the ministries that are organized through the church, it ultimately must be the vision of the church that determines the reason for its existence and how it functions in the community. It is important that a church doesn't add more programs simply because other churches have found them to be useful or because someone has their own agenda of what should be done. Too often churches get bogged down by that kind of process. To think organically, and in a manner consistent with postmodern culture, churches need to begin with a clear, biblically and theologically-grounded sense of vision. To summarize, a church's culture consists of its underlying values, and those values determine the church's sense of vision and vice-versa. It is vision that drives mission, and mission determines the kinds of services that begin to emerge to fulfill the vision.

Pastoral Care

If the development of vision is the prophetic role of a pastor, then pastoral care is his priestly function. This vital role of a pastor's ministry involves what we might think of as the "personal touch." It is well summed up in what it means for the pastor to be a shepherd to his people. It is, in many ways, the most prominent biblical image of what it means to be a pastor. In fact, the word "pastor" is derived from the very idea of a shepherd. To be a pastor means to be a shepherd.

This is the way in which Jesus thought of his own ministry in relation to his disciples and those to whom he came to share the good news of the kingdom. In Matthew 9:36, we read that "*When he saw the crowds, he had compassion for them, because they were harassed and helpless, like sheep without a shepherd.*" It was this image that constituted his sense of vision, as described earlier. His whole life and ministry were devoted to becoming a shepherd to those who recognized their need, to gather them into his fold, and to be their all-sufficient God. Shepherding speaks powerfully to his ministry of individual care, something reflected so beautifully in his famous talk in John 10 about being the Good Shepherd and giving his life for the sheep. We read there that he calls each by name and they follow him, because they recognize his voice and experience his special care.

It is this ministry of individualized and group care that I think is vital to a pastor's ministry, and that has special significance in these postmodern times. Amidst today's philosophical and practical chaos, due to the self-centered focus that has ensued, there is a profound sense of loss of personal identity and significance. If ever there was a time in which people find themselves "harassed and helpless," surely it must be in these confusing times. This situation represents a great opportunity for the church, the gospel, and meaningful pastoral ministry. People desperately need to know that they matter, not only for the benefit of the larger community, but for the sake of their own individual value.

I have learned that it's very important for the pastor to like people. It's one thing to feel a responsibility to love people despite their shortcomings, but it's quite another to find oneself attracted to people simply because they are beautifully made in God's image and have such wonderful gifts to share with the rest of the world. Pastors need to be willing to get to know their people, to hear their individual stories, and to learn to call them by their personal names. In this process, they need to learn how to be good listeners.

One of the most helpful bits of encouragement from Peter Scazzero's book, *The Emotionally Healthy Church*, is the short section on learning how to become a good listener. In that section, he writes about reflective listening, validation, and, exploring. Exploring is simply a matter of learning how to ask good questions, especially in the face of disagreement of one kind or another. A good deal of heated conflict can be avoided if there is a commitment to reflective listening, an exercise in which you repeat what you think you heard the other person say, without trying to make a judgement about it. Validation is a way of expressing support even when you may disagree. Scazzero writes:

> When I began to listen—really listen—to the people's stories and hearts, many of them cried. They felt valued, worthy, and loved. Initially it was difficult not to give advice or to react when I became uncomfortable...[47]

Though it includes it, pastoral care is about much more than simply paying attention to people in a time of crisis or some rite of passage. Critical care of that nature is important, but pastoral care is about demonstrating to people on a personal level that they truly do matter.

Of course, it's impossible for pastors to provide true, ongoing pastoral care for a lot of people—someone has suggested "more than fifty." Besides his own example, I think the pastor needs to ensure that there is a culture of care in the church community and beyond. Obviously, some people are more gifted in this kind of ministry than others, but everyone in the church can learn how to value others and provide focused attention in their connection with others. Often, especially in larger churches, it's possible for people to go in and out of worship services repeatedly without ever being acknowledged, greeted in a truly personal way, or included in the church-life experience.

---

47 Peter Scazzero, *The Emotionally Healthy Church*, (Grand Rapids, MI: Zondervan, 2003), 183.

Ministries should develop so that mutual care is an important element of a church's existence. As people work together on other service projects, care for one another becomes a natural part of their relationships, but it's also important for leaders to become intentional about this aspect of their work. Otherwise, people may begin to feel like they don't matter as much as the project or work that is being undertaken. A pastoral care emphasis ensures that they really do matter.

Administrative Leadership

Another key essential of effective pastoral ministry concerns what I think of as administrative leadership. It consists of developing and managing ministries based on the vision that has been established. At first, this sounds like something more peculiar to the "modern era," since it implies some degree of organizational structure. But it isn't necessary to abandon all elements of organization simply because one is seeking to be an effective pastor in postmodern times.

It's true that the postmodern mindset is less formal and more spontaneous. People like to do what's meaningful in the moment rather than continually having to conform to existing structures. Nevertheless, success doesn't just happen. It usually is the outcome of a plan which is a biblical concept (i.e. Proverbs 16:3). And while postmodern structures will look different because they are less of an end in themselves, it still is important for structures to exist that can effectively facilitate the fulfillment of a vision.

Often in postmodern times, organization is built on a relational paradigm instead of a hierarchal one. This means that the emphasis is less on formal leadership than it is on teams—people working together in a common cause. Inevitably, of course, this does require leadership, but that leadership will look a lot different today than it did twenty or thirty years ago. A large part of effective ministry in the church of today is in the development of teams who are led by people who work intentionally, even though they may have a pretty low profile otherwise.

One of the main responsibilities of a pastor is to develop these kinds of leaders and teams. This is essential, because it is impossible to accomplish very much of anything at all by one's own effort. This is why Jesus made such a huge commitment in his earthly ministry to the calling and equipping of disciples. He had a strong sense of vision to complete a unique task, which was the establishment of the church (Matthew 16:18). He did this partially through his public speaking, teaching, and healing ministry. But to complete the task, he knew that it would require the engagement of others who would understand his vision and how to accomplish it.

As Jesus' method was to choose, train, and commission certain ones (whom he called disciples) to go and make more disciples (as defined in the Great Commission, Matthew 28:19– 20), so it is of primary importance for leaders in the church universally to like-wise recruit, equip, and send out "Jesus followers." In the early church, the disciples of Jesus made this function a large part of their ministry. We read of Paul (a later disciple) recruiting, training, and commissioning Timothy, for example. In 2 Timothy 2:2, he writes to him, "*... what you have heard from me in the presence of many witnesses entrust to faithful men, who will be able to teach others also.*" In his letter to the Ephesians, which largely consists of instructions concerning the nature of the church, Paul writes that in Jesus' ascension after his death and resurrection, he gave certain gifts of service to the church, including pastors and teachers:

> ...to equip the saints for the work of ministry,
> for building up the body of Christ, until we all
> attain to the unity of the faith and knowledge
> of the Son of God, to mature manhood, to the
> measure of the stature of the fullness of Christ ...
> (Ephesians 4:12–13)

Much of what true leadership in the church is all about concerns the fine art of training those who are called to Christ and then helping them find their place of service in the church and Christ's kingdom. This is true administrative leadership. It is not, as is so often supposed, simply a bureaucratic role of "shuffling paper and filling out reports," a modern view of administration. That too is important work, but it should not primarily be the work of the pastor. A huge part of a lead pastor's work, however, does have to do with developing leaders. I've observed that women are often especially gifted in this kind of practical administrative leadership, sometimes considered to be the biblical work of deacons (as in the possible case of Phoebe – Romans 16:1). In my view, it's one possible way for women to be employed in the church.

The focus on developing leaders ideally should not be simply to find occupants for programs or ministry leadership roles. Though that may be one consideration, the real stuff of leadership development has to do with identifying spiritual gifts within the church body and then encouraging their development by participation in a learning and ministry team. Team leadership, I believe, is one of the best ways to describe how ministries ought to function in the church. It consists of a properly identified leader, recruiting and engaging other called ones in a community of learning and service for the sake of their own development while also accomplishing a larger ministry purpose.

It is important, therefore, to consider that a pastor's identifiable success is not simply about his pulpit speaking ability and practice (even though that will be very important), but even more about his ability to develop and lead an array of ministry teams. I have often considered that one of my greatest joys in pastoral ministry is seeing ministry multiplied through the effective development of team leaders. In that sense, so much of effective pastoral ministry consists of passing on the privilege of service leadership to others. Unquestionably, from the perspective of pastoral methodology, this is one of the prime factors in church ministry development and success.

This process of ministry team development begins with the selection of those who are called to serve on the leadership team of the entire church (commonly identified as the Board of Elders or Deacons). Wisely so, often the selection of these leaders is a shared process in the sense that mature church members are involved with the pastor in this (annual) process. The pastor's relationship and work with the main leadership team of the church is vital to everything else that develops in the life and ministry of a church. This approach avoids the common mistake of thinking of the church Board as a corporate business leadership group. In my view, it is essential that the pastor and Board members work together as a spiritual leadership team under the pastor's coaching role. Their qualification and selection is of the utmost importance in the life of the church. Of course, there will be times when the Board will necessarily function as the pastor's employer, as in the case, of conducting a formal (annual) evaluation of the pastor's ministry. But such roles for the Board should only take place at pre-determined times and in necessary circumstances. Even regular financial reports at the Board level, for instance, ought to be dealt with in the context of the entire team's discussion about the larger ministry and vision of the church.

In former, modern times, the relationship of the Board to the pastor tended to be much more formal, perhaps even corporate. In this paradigm, unfortunately, it wasn't uncommon for a sense of acrimony to develop between the pastor and Board. Quite unbiblically, it often turned out to be a competitive relationship—the pastor seeking to direct by presenting his ideas while being opposed by the members of the Board (or vice versa). Though this kind of discordant relationship can still happen in these times, I sense that pastors want to lead the Board in ways that are much more organic. It's commendable that Boards and pastors think of themselves much more as a spiritual body of leaders rather than executives of a corporation. This seems much more in keeping with the biblical image of the Elders and pastor as shepherds of God's flock (Acts 20:28, 1 Peter 5:1–5). It is a refreshing change from what seemed to be the case in the more "modern" period. This topic could be its own book, but at least this is an introduction to the subject of leadership in the church.

The call to make disciples then, I think, is essentially a kind of administrative role in which the pastor takes responsibility to teach the members of the church to know what it means to be followers of Jesus. But it also involves equipping individuals, as they spiritually mature, to find their place of service in the body of Christ or the work of God's kingdom, according to their gifts. In many ways, it turns out that this may be the most exciting work of all in true pastoral ministry.

Evangelism and Mission

Evangelism and mission are related to the earlier-mentioned matter of vision. Because one of the essential elements in successful church ministry in postmodern times has to do with how a church, under its leadership, addresses and fulfills Christ's mission. It used to be, especially in the modern era, that churches could be satisfied, to put it simply, with some sort of local evangelism program and an overseas mission program. Mission(s) was something that trained missionaries did cross-culturally and overseas. Evangelism was a local focus of the church. Pastors found ways to do evangelism through preaching, counselling, and visiting people connected with the church. Church members were taught how to share the main points of the gospel and invite people to respond in faith.

As I mentioned earlier, there used to be a large variety of evangelism programs, including "crusade" evangelism and various means of "personal" evangelism. Some of the more popular ones used methods like *The Four Spiritual Laws*, the *Bridge Illustration*, *The Roman Road*, *Evangelism Explosion*, and *The Way of the Master*. These methods emphasized the importance of individual salvation. Elements in the gospel presentation included the nature of God as just and holy (but also loving), man's separation from God because of sin, the ultimate consequence of sin in terms of death and eternal separation from God (including hell), God's remedy through Jesus' atoning sacrifice and resurrection, and the need for a personal response of faith in order to have assurance of salvation. Simple faith, expressed through a genuine prayer of confessing one's sin and trusting Christ for salvation, was emphasized as a contrast to seeking salvation through some meritorious "works" approach (i.e. Ephesians 2:8–9).

In the modern period, among evangelical churches, evangelism was understood as sharing the good news of God's salvation offer in Jesus and inviting people to respond. Undoubtedly, many thousands and probably even millions of people were genuinely converted and "saved" by this means. Since the Bible speaks often of spiritual regeneration or the experience of "new birth" (Ezekiel 36:26–27; John 3:3–8; Titus 3:5–6; 1 Peter 1:3), many identified their conversion experience as an event at a particular moment in time (just as in physical birth) when they came to believe in this way.

As a young child, I came to true assurance of a relationship with God by this kind of response. I can still remember the day and the circumstances in which I felt God's definite call "to be saved." Using scriptures like John 3:16, Ephesians 2:8–9, Romans 3:23, 6:23, and 10:9–10, my mother explained the gospel to me as outlined here. In a simple prayer, I confessed faith in Christ and trusted him to come into my life. Based on the biblical promise (John 3:16, 1 John 5:10–14), I have lived my whole life with a deep sense of assurance concerning my relationship with God. Later, as an extension of my initial faith, I was baptized and progressively came to understand what it meant to be a disciple of Jesus Christ.

Under the gradual cultural change towards postmodernism, this earlier view of the simplicity of the gospel has certainly taken a turn. Through the influence of writers like Scott McKnight, Brian McLaren, N. T. Wright, and others (as mentioned earlier) the gospel has come to be described more in terms of one's response to the announcement of the arrival of Jesus' kingdom, instead of a personal response of Jesus' death and resurrection for the forgiveness of sin.

In his book, *Center Church*, Tim Keller does a good job, I think, of describing how and why this change came about. He speaks of how the Latin phrase, *missio Dei* (the mission of God), captured the initial idea of what being a missional church was all about. He suggests that it grew out of Karl Barth's emphasis on the idea that the church needs to become a participant in what God is already doing in the world to redeem creation. Barth's ideas have moved the evangelical church from an emphasis on individual salvation, to Christian influence in the secular world.[48]

Another influential thinker on recent evangelical ideas of mission has been Lesslie Newbigin. He served as a missionary and churchman in India and England in the last century, and for a time as the general secretary of the World Council of Churches. Newbigin never fully identified as an evangelical because of its strong commitment to biblical authority, the atonement, and individual salvation-focus of the gospel. Yet many evangelicals, it seems, have been interested in his larger understanding of church mission as culturally transformational. Newbigin's views of the nature of the gospel and the church's mission are summed up in this:

> The church is the bearer to all nations of a gospel that announces the kingdom, the reign, and the sovereignty of God. It calls men and women to repent of their false loyalty to other powers, to become believers in the one true sovereignty, and so to become corporately a sign, instrument, and foretaste of that sovereignty of the one true and living God over all nature, all nations, and all human lives. It is not meant to call men and women out of the world into a safe religious

---

48 Tim Keller, *Center Church: Doing Balanced, Gospel-Centered Ministry in Your City* (Grand Rapids: Zondervan, 2012), 251.

enclave but to call them out in order to send them
back as agents of God's kingship.[49]

Writers such as Newbigin and others have encouraged a greater
emphasis among evangelicals in these postmodern times on the
mission of the church as a way that also includes the pursuit of
social justice. Much of this, I believe, is also tied to amillennial ideas
concerning eschatology, especially in relation to the meaning of the
coming of Christ's kingdom. (Amillennialism is a way of interpreting scripture that treats references to the millennium in Revelation
20 figuratively instead of literally. It implies that the Kingdom of
God is already here through the first coming of Christ, and that
prophecies concerning national Israel have already been fulfilled in
the church.) As in the case of Newbigin, many in these postmodern
times are inclined to believe that part of what it means to spread the
good news is to announce the coming of Christ's kingdom and to
engage in the world with a view towards cultural transformation.
Though the literal return of Jesus Christ is affirmed, there often
seems to be less assurance about what this may entail, and a greater
emphasis on the responsibility of the church to usher in this reality.

I'm inclined to think that some of this redefinition of church
mission has been partly due to the current secular culture's emotional reaction to the church's gospel message of salvation from
God's judgement through faith in Christ. Consistent with the
popular notions of tolerance and pluralism, Christians are being
challenged about their genuine sense of care for people whose
views and attitudes often conflict with theirs. It's a challenge that
calls Christians to think more deeply about mission beyond the

---

49 Lesslie Newbigin, *Foolishness to the Greeks: The Gospel and Western
Culture*, (Grand Rapids, MI: Eerdmans, 1986), 124.

traditional understanding of evangelism, yet it's important that the essential nature of the gospel as it relates to personal salvation continues to be central to what mission is all about.

This also seems to be the burden of recent leading evangelicals such as Tim Keller. He writes that:

> ... missional churches must equip laypeople both for evangelistic witness and for public life and vocation ... our mission cannot go forward without Christians being involved not only in calling people to conversion but also in service to the community and in doing justice ... most missional thinkers agree that the witness of the Christians must be in both word and deed.[50]

Keller goes on to write passionately about the danger, in these times, of losing the essential meaning of the gospel as good news about individual salvation through faith in the atoning work of Christ. He's concerned that missional church terminology easily tends to emphasize the corporate or horizontal dimension of faith to the exclusion of the classic doctrines of sin and of our individual accountability before a holy God whose wrath has been propitiated in Jesus' substitutionary atonement.[51] His conclusion is that the gospel concerning individual salvation through faith in Christ's atonement is essential to an understanding of what is involved in being a missional church. He affirms that its effective communication will take a different form than it did in former times. By its very nature, that communication will also entail real engagement

---

50   Keller, *Center Church*, 259.

51   Keller, *Center Church*, 267.

with secular culture, both individually and corporately, with a view to true service for Christ.[52]

An essential element in successful church ministry in postmodern times is thinking through and working out a proactive philosophy of evangelism and church mission. The most effective approach, no doubt, will retain a clear understanding of the nature of the gospel with a view to how it may be authentically communicated, individually and corporately, primarily in word, but also in deed. This conviction will go a long way to informing the vision of any local church, enabling it, by the grace of Jesus Christ and the power of the Holy Spirit, to fulfill God's redemptive will.

The postmodern reality of today's Western world requires clear thinking about the true nature of pastoral leadership and church ministry. Church ministry today requires pastoral leaders who experience and live out what can only be described as biblical authenticity. Their ministry needs to be compelled by a clear sense of biblical vision for the people of their churches and community. They must be shepherds to their people in every way the word implies. They need to have strong leadership skills in discipling, recruiting and training other potential leaders based on their spiritual gifts, and then forming them into teams whose members know how to care for one another and how to effectively complete the practical tasks they have been assigned. And the vision and leadership of today's pastors needs to be informed by a deep conviction about the critical nature of the gospel and how best to communicate it in these times to truly build the church and expand Christ's kingdom.

---

52   Ibid., 271–274.

CHAPTER 10

Evangelical Commitment for Postmodern Times

The rapid shift towards postmodernism in the last four or five decades has meant profound changes for the world, for Western culture, and for the Christian church. In this book, I have tried to document, in some small way, the nature and reason for this shift. I have been especially interested in its impact on the church in which I have had some small opportunity to serve through these years. During this relatively short period of time, we have seen a profound move away from traditional evangelical practice. Some of those changes have appeared to be rather superficial in a simple effort to do things that seem to align more readily with similar, seemingly harmless expressions, in the surrounding culture. At the same time, it is increasingly evident that changes in evangelical practice have been prompted by a true revolution happening at a much deeper philosophical and sociological level.

As has been liberally emphasized at the beginning of this book, change is not only inevitable, but also capable of generating new and better understandings about ways of living. Besides, Christians believe that there is a sovereign Hand that is actively guiding the affairs of the natural world, of human history, and of the world's redemption. As Christians, we have the privilege and responsibility of trying to discern the nature of change in all of these spheres from God's perspective, and then also in seeking to align our lives with God's will in the midst of them.

The problem is that we may easily fall prey to Satan's objective to thwart God's redemptive plan by misunderstanding what God is doing, all the while actively resisting the changes that God is seeking to use for his own ends. One effect of this resistance is a variety of unhealthy reactions. On one level, we may become angry (righteously so, we think) and begin to attack those (usually in the church) whom we believe are promoting the change. In the worst of cases, we may simply withdraw from further engagement. But disengagement can lead to wasteful distractions and, possibly, the loss of faith. Unintentionally, withdrawal plays into the hands of the devil, who is actively going about seeking to destroy the work of Christ.

Another alternative, and the one I am suggesting in this book, is to try to understand the reason for the profound changes that we have seen in the church, to discern which are misleading, and to embrace a deeper conviction of how the authentic gospel can continue to have the transformational effect that God intended. In the context of the reality of the Christian church's continuing struggle with secular culture, it is important to understand how the gospel is still *"the power of God for salvation to everyone that believes,"* (Romans 1:16). It is my conviction that what is needed today is a greater understanding than ever of the truth and relevance of the gospel.

In its long history, the Christian church has endured many distractions, aberrations, and outright attacks. This reality was captured so artistically many years ago in Samuel Stone's hymn, "The Church's One Foundation." The third and fourth stanzas expound:

Though with a scornful wonder,
Men see her sore oppressed,
By schisms rent asunder,
By heresies distressed,
Yet saints their watch are keeping;
Their cry goes up— "How long?"
But soon the night of weeping
Shall be the morn of song.

'Mid toil and tribulation
And tumult of her war,
She waits the consummation
Of peace forevermore;
Till with the vision glorious
Her longing eyes are blest,
And the great Church victorious
Shall be the Church at rest.

It's a testimony to the unwavering truth of God's existence and his plan in Christ that the church has withstood all the world's changes and various pressures, continuing to grow and develop through the years, decades, and centuries. Radical philosophical change is not new to the church, and it's something that God, in his sovereignty, has often used to his advantage again and again.

One has only to think of God's timing in the revelation of Jesus Christ to the world during the era of the Greek and Roman empires. Greek philosophy and language paved the way for an articulation of the gospel message in a way that was ideal for clarity and influence. The vastness and sophistication of the Roman Empire in that time made it possible for the more rapid dissemination of the message. Consistent with the rise of the Age of Reason in the middle of the second millennium, the rationale of the Reformation offered important corrections to a church that had become increasingly side-tracked, conflicted, corrupted, and even abusive. It's as though, in his sovereignty and grace, God took advantage of these secular changes to ensure the best possible outcome concerning his intentions to build the church and expand his kingdom.

While some may feel that the postmodern development of our times might easily lead toward the diminution of the church, there is no doubt in my mind that God is capable of creatively using this situation and these times to greatly enhance the work of his kingdom and the building of his church. Though we can't be sure how that might happen, it's possible that the current climate of skepticism could lead to a deeper yearning for true spiritual reality, prompting genuine prayer and a Christian revival. Prayer is what characterized the spiritual revivals during the times of the judges, like Gideon, Deborah, and Samuel. As God's people cried out to him amid their oppression from surrounding evil-hearted neighbours, he heard their prayers and sent them a deliverer. It's been noted that prayer was also a major factor in the spiritual revivals in the West in the eighteenth and nineteenth centuries.

Centrality of the Gospel

Another possible result of the secularization of our times, and consistent with the previous idea, could be a clarification of the meaning and significance of biblical authority and of the very nature of the gospel. It seems to me that, however it comes about, this development is essential to the church's recovery of strength and courage in this time. It is only in the context of these convictions that the church can ever hope to have the influence God intends. It is for this reason that I have tried, in simple language, to describe something of the philosophical shift that has taken place. I believe we need to recognize the basic elements of this change, how it has affected the church for evil and for good, and what needs to be done for the church to persevere in its calling.

If one studies the development of the work and ministry of the early church in the New Testament, something that becomes immediately evident is that it grew so quickly because of the focus on the gospel. It was the spreading of the gospel, I believe, which was the primary focus of the Holy Spirit after he was sent by Jesus to be with the new believers and to empower them for ministry (Acts 2). The gospel concerning Jesus was certainly the subject of the apostles' preaching and teaching ministry after the Spirit came. Their works of healing and acts of compassion were intimately related to the fact of Jesus's coming, to his death and resurrection for the forgiveness of sin, and to his teachings about how to live in love and truth.

When Paul came along a little bit later to supplement the work of the other apostles, his conversion and calling not only demonstrated the ultimate profound effect of the gospel, but focused even more clearly on the gospel as *the* truth that could literally change the world. His whole letter to the Romans, for example, is all about the true message of the gospel and how it can bring the kind of change in people's lives that reflects true salvation from sin's judgement and power. Though response to the gospel was sure to have a social impact, time and again we see in Paul's letters (as well as those of the other apostles) that the gospel is about individual response and conversion.

Galatians is another of Paul's letters that is directed at defending the truth and nature of the gospel, especially in a Jewish context. Paul often speaks about a very defined body of knowledge when he writes about "the gospel of Christ" and the preaching of "a gospel contrary to the one we preached to you" (Galatians 1:7–8). That gospel is all about one's justification before God (and all its permutations), centered in the atonement event of Christ's crucifixion, coupled with his resurrection. Elsewhere (1 Timothy 2:4–6), Paul writes about God's desire for the salvation of all people through the knowledge of the truth regarding the exclusive mediation "*between God and men*" through Christ, "*who gave himself as a ransom for all, which is the testimony given at the proper time.*"

Repeatedly, Paul defines the gospel in terms of the salvation provided through Christ for those who believe. Peter also writes about this, as in 1 Peter 3:18, where he speaks of Christ suffering once for sins, "*the righteous for the unrighteous, that he might bring us to God, being put to death in the flesh but made alive in the spirit.*" By various terms, all the apostles refer to the gospel as a specific revelation concerning Jesus—his coming, his salvation from sin through his death and resurrection, and the benefits that accrue through faith in him that also includes the impartation of his Spirit and inauguration into his eternal kingdom.

A church's understanding of the nature of the gospel is vital to the reason for its existence and activity. Because the gospel is permeated with such rich variety, it's possible for churches to emphasize only one part of it at the expense of its essential meaning. In his book, *Center Church*, Tim Keller aptly delineates the nature of the gospel so that churches, their leaders, and members don't become confused about what's important. For clearer understanding about this important matter, I would recommend a study of a couple of chapters from his book called, "Center Church," in which he writes about the nature of the gospel.[53]

---

53 Tim Keller, *Center Church*, 27 - 44.

Once a church understands the essential meaning of the gospel in terms of God's revelation in Christ, his death and resurrection for the forgiveness of our sins, and the gift of eternal life, it can go on to consider the best ways to try and communicate the good news of Jesus in these times. Any effort to do so will necessarily prove to be both simple and highly complex. It may involve everything from a simple testimony of faith to an apologetic of the Christian faith. It's important that churches design strategies and educate their members on how to effectively communicate the Good News in these times. This can take many different forms, of course, but for churches to be viable and strong in the current cultural milieu, it is imperative that they give careful thought to the matter of how to do this intentionally, with courage and sensitivity. With this in mind, I would like to provide an introduction to some ideas by which it may be possible for churches and their individual members to design appropriate strategies and approaches about how to share the Good News in these times.

Individual Christian Witness to the Gospel

One of the first considerations is that the church and Christians, because of the gospel's centrality to the Christian faith, determine to be intentional about its communication. So often, especially in view of the subtle forms of discrimination that can exist today, it's easy for Christians to assume a more or less passive attitude about sharing the gospel. Sometimes their default in communicating with non-believers may be to speak about peripheral matters. In the worst of cases, a defensive posture in sharing the Good News could easily take the form of avoiding secular people, of spending most of one's time with fellow believers, or of focusing all of one's time and energy entirely on work and recreation. Another form of this avoidance is to satisfy oneself with the development of ministries within the church itself. But for Christians to engage with people outside of the church concerning the gospel, they must begin with a deep sense of appreciation for the incredible beauty and richness of the gospel and that it is the only means by which anyone can experience God's salvation.

Once a church and its members have established that this kind of communication is important, the next level of commitment entails finding ways to build relationships with people in one's immediate community who do not necessarily have a connection to the Christian faith—neighbours, work associates, recreational connections, school friends, and even members of one's extended family. Integration with people in one's community is essential to gospel communication, but, this must be genuine, not simply because of an agenda to share the gospel.

Just yesterday, I read of a church in Tallahassee, Florida that is bucking the trend of young adults' departure from church participation. In answer to the question of how they have built such a large church from the participation of college students, their response is:

> Our evangelism strategy is relationships: Open
> your eyes to the people already in front of you
> at work, in the dorm, and on your baseball team.
> Creating Christian alternatives is not how we
> operate; our students are encouraged to be as

"in the world" as possible while maintaining
Christian distinction. [54]

Essentially, the decision to relate to people outside of the church
through relationships should be based on the conviction that people
really do matter. One must determine to see people the way God
himself sees them and cares about them. It's true that there will
always be risks of hurt in any relationship because of people's spiritually fallen condition. But in order to relate the gospel to people,
one must be attracted to them as God is and to love them for his
sake. Often as you begin to practice this, you discover that people
have qualities and abilities from which you can learn and benefit a
great deal. In fact, one way to grow in relationship with others is to
ask interesting questions about their lives and abilities with a view
to appreciating the diverse beauty of God's creation. In becoming
a good listener, a Christian may discover points of connection that
will enable him or her to begin to introduce God's great story of
good news in Christ.

It's impossible to have a relationship with anyone for long
without learning something of their values and spiritual beliefs.
It usually isn't long before you end up sharing something of your
own identity, including your values and what you believe. In my
own case, this happens quite quickly in a new relationship simply
because I have worked in pastoral church ministry most of my life.

---

54 Daniel Darling, "Most College Students are Leaving the Church; Here's
How This Church is Bucking the Trend," *Christianity Today: The Local
Church*, October 20, 2016, accessed on January 4, 2017, https://church-
healthwiki.wordpress.com/2016/10/21/oikos-evangelism-most-
college-students-are-leaving-the-church-heres-how-this-congregation-
is-bucking-the-trend/.

In my airline travels, for example, I have had many conversations that soon develop into discussions about faith. After listening and asking questions, I often will have an opportunity to speak briefly about my own spiritual journey and why I have come to believe in Jesus Christ. Since these conversations are often brief, they don't usually result in long relationships, or even in conversions, but the experience illustrates how social connections can easily lead to opportunities to discuss issues of faith.

Sometimes because most of my work is in the church, I find myself having to make a special effort to connect with people who aren't part of my faith-based circle of friendships. This usually moves me in a direction of interest or need that I already have. For example, because I have a need for physical recreation, I like to go to the gym to work out or to play the game of squash. So often, especially through squash, I have had the opportunity to meet people outside of the church. A while ago I went to play squash on my own, and soon found myself meeting someone at the squash courts who had recently immigrated from another country. He was interested in learning how to play the game. Though I am not an expert in squash, I was able to teach him the basics of the game, and soon we were playing together regularly. It wasn't long before he became a proficient squash player, quickly passing my skills. But the best part was the experience of our friendship that blossomed into a deep discussion about matters of faith. Even before my work in that place was finished and I moved on, he and his wife developed friendships with others from the church.

One of the beautiful realities of life in a postmodern world is that relationships develop best through natural means. This newer development is an extension of the current western culture's interest in that which is authentic and organic. For me, this means that I can be myself. I don't have to feel any pressure to even bring up the subject of faith if it doesn't seem to fit. I can wait for the inner promptings of the Spirit to lead the conversation in ways that will affirm others, even if it seems they aren't ready to talk about matters of faith. But I also keep looking for opportunities, listening to promptings of the Spirit, to talk about personal values that might lead to a discussion about the Christian faith.

A person's discovery of Christ and his gospel doesn't necessarily depend upon one encounter. In fact, most people who become Christians these days come through a whole series of exposures to various elements in the gospel. It may involve encounters with a large variety of people who are also Christians. Seeing faith-development as a process is a helpful way of understanding the work of evangelism. Years ago, this was very well illustrated by Engel's Scale, called *Steps to Christ*. James Engel proposed a series of steps from unawareness of God to an actual decision of faith. He also developed a scale for growth and development after conversion. It's a helpful concept, even though it's not likely that one's journey these days will be as methodical as the illustration suggests. But the point is well-taken that faith is often a process that begins with some minimal positive exposure that begins a journey of increased desire and knowledge about what it means to be a Christian.

Keller suggests a similar process in several steps that he identifies which begin to answer obvious questions for a person as they come in contact with Christians: awareness, relevance, credibility, trial, commitment, and reinforcement.[55] The relationship with Christians, especially over a prolonged period, will naturally lead to opportunities to talk about biblical themes and the gospel. Presenting the gospel itself needn't be a tight formal presentation

---

55   Keller, 281 - 282.

that could easily appear like a sermon. It's best these days, I think, to talk about it in terms of God's larger story.

For example, there may be an occasion to say something like this: *You know, I've come to the conclusion that the biblical story is very credible. It explains the beauty of the world in terms of a perfect and powerful Creator. It also explains why there is so much that is less than perfect and downright evil in the world. But the biggest biblical story of all, I think, is how God reached out to the world in the coming of Jesus, who was the perfect human in every way. By his cruel death and then his resurrection, he became God's love sacrifice to the world so that anyone of us can experience an actual relationship with God. Opening my life to the God of the Bible and coming to truly believe in his Son, Jesus Christ, has come to mean everything to me...* The essentials in this bit of gospel communication include the biblical foundation, creation, the existence of evil and suffering, the significance of Jesus, his death and resurrection, and the place of faith.

There are many ways to communicate these basics of the gospel story, but it begins to give you an idea of how this can be done very simply in these times. There are also many variables as to the kind of response one might receive to such a simple explanation at the right time. But it's a start and might produce a series of questions that would progressively lead to more discussion or study. It's a way of telling one's own story without being judgemental or preachy. After a relationship has been established, it would likely be well-received. It could also lead to some resistance or argument, but that need not lead to the end of a relationship. In fact, sometimes a small reference to the gospel story might go further by including a question about what your friend thinks about these things. If she or he is interested, it could lead to a short prayer that calls on God for his salvation through faith in Christ. If this happens, it is important to explain the basis of assurance for a relationship with God based on faith (Romans 10:9–10, 1 John 5:11–12).

It's important to recognize that while the nature of gospel ministry is expansive enough to also include all manner of deeds done in the name of Christ, evangelism itself is ultimately about sharing the good news about the saving work of Jesus Christ for the forgiveness of sin and full participation in his kingdom. It is Christian witness to this body of truth that makes it possible to lead people to the assurance of saving faith. It is for this reason, I believe, that a church's culture must be formed with this purpose in mind.

Church Ministry Surrounding Gospel Witness

Church life and ministry needs to be geared, I think, towards creating a culture that surrounds the meaning and communication of the gospel. This means that an emphasis and understanding of the gospel concerning Jesus must be central to all that the church is about. Because the ministry of the church is complex, it's easy for its leaders and members to become involved in many things that often may be quite peripheral to a gospel focus. But if the vision of the church is centered in the truth of the gospel and its communication, then all its ministries can be structured to see that its propagation remains the priority and the very reason for its existence. If gospel-centered ministry is the focus, then ministries can be evaluated on those terms.

I believe church leaders are responsible to keep the vision clear and to create a culture that surrounds that vision. Preaching should be geared to illuminate the truth of the gospel in the context of the whole Bible in such a way that both those who believe and those who are seeking can see that Jesus has come to impart true life to all who believe. It seems this was Saint Paul's method in the letters that he wrote to the churches. He would start with an explanation or defense of the gospel and then demonstrate how it affects every aspect of life. (See his letter to the Ephesians, for example.)

Church worship should be planned in a way that makes it possible for all in attendance to experience the very presence of Christ. Through the songs, prayers, biblical liturgy, testimonials, fellowship (even the congregational updates), and preaching, participants in the worship service should be able to relate to the gospel both cognitively and emotionally. They should be able to access the grace of Christ for their own personal need as they also come to understand more of God's plan and purposes in the good news concerning Jesus, according to the scriptures.

An explanation that speaks to the emotional needs that people feel in relation to God is an important place to start in these times, rather than providing one that merely seeks to provide a logical reason for people to believe. This is the point of Tim Keller's recent book, *Making Sense of God*. Before people are ready to consider rational arguments for faith, they need to have their basic feelings addressed about injustice in the world, inequality, and why, for example, a materialistic view of the world is inadequate.

While the worship services reflect a large part of a church's culture, it's really about a lot more than happens in those services. It also concerns how people in the church relate to one another, how their spiritual gifts are identified and used, how its ministries are purposed and organized, and how the church relates to the larger community in which it exists. If a church's culture is centered in the truth of the Bible and the gospel, then it's all about how its people relate to each other and others in the light of that truth. It is a pastoral issue for the church that its people learn to truly love one another, care for one another, and serve one another out of appreciation for the truth of the gospel.

Evangelism should be taught in the context of the meaning of the gospel so that it is practiced organically. But it also is something that can be organized and promoted as the members of the church demonstrate spiritual maturity and leadership skills in their understanding and practice of gospel truth. There is much concerning the truth and practice of the gospel that can be learned and experienced in the context of small groups of the church that meet outside of the larger weekly worship times. It is the responsibility of church leaders to multiply the life and ministry of Christ in the church through identifying and encouraging what is sometimes referred to as lay leadership development.

A third layer of church culture development around the gospel, I think, concerns how churches prepare their members to relate to people outside of their immediate Christian communities. Christians need education, training, and organizing in understanding and strategizing that can help them relate to non-believers with gospel-thinking in mind. Christians need to be taught about the supreme importance of God's love and care for others without any kind of discrimination whatsoever concerning their identity, dispositions, and activities. Because of the reality and nature of the gospel, they need to be encouraged to develop relationships organically with their neighbours in every context. They need to understand their neighbours' great value, despite their sinfulness (just as their own), from God's perspective. They need teaching, I think, about how to live as followers of Jesus in these relationships and contexts, and also how to represent the gospel, both in deed and word.

In my view, church leaders should take responsibility to teach church members about how to be fluent in every aspect of the language of the gospel with their non-Christian associates. This includes how to answer common critical questions about the Christian faith—God's existence, creation versus evolution, the reliability of the Bible, the reason for suffering, why there are universally acknowledged standards of morality, and so on. But it's also a good idea for them to organize some activities that involve their members in deeds of service to the community, as well as in specific ministries that engage people in an understanding of the gospel.

Too often, churches do gospel work continuously without any reference to gospel truth. They feel it is enough to offer a cup of cold water in Jesus's name (Matthew 10:42). This obviously has some merit in the fulfillment of God's larger plan, but ultimately gospel ministries of the church should lead towards an understanding of the content of the gospel so that people can hear and respond to it. A gospel-centered church will inevitably develop strategies that serve the practical needs of people in a community, but with a view also to providing answers in gospel truth from questions that arise. Ministries of justice and compassion through various kinds of practical services such as providing help for the sick and the poor should be designed in a way that point recipients to the wonder of who Jesus is and what he has come to do. It's notable that Jesus' own ministries of practical assistance were ultimately tied to his identity and teaching. (See John's Gospel, for example.) It is in these ways that people in any community may be introduced to the kingdom of Christ and ultimately the church.

The Church and the Kingdom

An important philosophical church ministry development for me has been an attempt to recognize somewhat of a distinction between what we understand as the kingdom of God and the church. Based on Jesus' references to the kingdom of God in the Gospels, it is evident that Christ's kingdom is about his ever-increasing reign in a world that has been dominated by the "prince of this world" since the Fall (John 12:31). By Christ's coming and his death and resurrection, Jesus' kingdom of light was inaugurated and began to replace Satan's kingdom of darkness. Eventually, eschatologically speaking, the prince of darkness will be cast into hell, and Jesus will reign forever in a new heaven and a new earth (Revelation 11:15).

The church, on the other hand, could be thought of as a more formal expression of the kingdom of God. It comes as a later development out of the kingdom of God. It was initially established, as Jesus promised (Matthew 16:18), when he sent the Holy Spirit into the world upon the praying and waiting disciples in Jerusalem (Acts 2). The church was to exist as a specific and leading expression of what the kingdom of God was all about. Entrance into the kingdom, according to Jesus' words in John's Gospel (John 3:3–7), comes by way of faith and includes regeneration (or new birth). Faith and the new birth are also foundational to entrance into, and identification with, Christ's church. But identification with the church is more fully established through baptism and participation in what is known as communion, or the Lord's Supper (1 Corinthians 11:23–32).

First and foremost, the church has a discipling ministry of teaching, training, and commissioning its members to become full participants in the expansion of Christ's kingdom. Church life and ministry itself entails a structure of formalized leadership, which has responsibility to give direction to the church, to teach, train, and sometimes offer correction to its members. The kingdom, on the other hand, is the more general work of Christ through the members of the church to represent him in the world by their presence, witness, and deeds. As the original Jewish tabernacle was a reflection of a heavenly tabernacle (Hebrews 8:5) and functioned as a model for the spiritual ministry in the community of God's people, it's also possible to think of the church now as a representation of the heavenly tabernacle and of Christ, with the purpose of conducting spiritual ministry for those who belong to Christ's kingdom. By this means, the kingdom continues to expand towards its full completion at the return of Christ.

While principles for the establishment of the church are laid down in the Gospels through the work and teaching of Christ, it is the apostles who are given more specific revelation of how the church was to function. Their most important work was to seek to establish churches through which God's greater kingdom work could be accomplished. Churches, in all their geographical locations, are really the institutional emissaries of the good news of the coming of Jesus, his salvation, and his eventual and eternal reign over all things. The church functions as a leader in God's larger kingdom work. The kingdom is the larger sphere of God's activity in the world by which he increasingly becomes known and demonstrates his presence and power.

It is in this sense that the role and ministry of the church is somewhat distinct from God's kingdom ministry in the world. In this regard, Tim Keller refers to the work of Geerhardus Vos, *The Teaching of Jesus Concerning the Kingdom of God and the Church.* He summarizes: "Vos teaches that the Kingdom of God mainly operates through the church, but that it also operates through

Christians who integrate their faith and their work."[56] Kingdom ministry is a more generic form of God's specific discipling ministry. It is important for followers of Jesus to be full participants in the worship, fellowship, discipling, and evangelizing ministry of the local church. But as they go about their work and other more generic ministries in the world, they should see themselves as being part of God's greater kingdom ministry in which he seeks to make his presence and influence known.

Consider, for example, all the ways in which Christ's influence is being experienced through humanitarian ministries conducted as Christian ministries or, at least in Jesus' name. Strictly speaking, these do not exist as church ministries. (Formerly, these were often spoken of as, "para-church ministries.") Reflect also on the large number of ways in which Christians are living out their lives and conducting their work in the world. As they do their work in Jesus' name in their various places of employment, they not only experience God's provision for their daily needs, but are also agents for good in the expansion of Christ's kingdom. Though there is resistance and outright opposition to the expansion of Christ's kingdom in many forms and places, it's amazing to see, in the world's history, how Christ's influence has grown. In Jesus' own words, it is like a mustard seed that a man took and planted in his field. It grew, not only to become *"the largest of garden plants, but a tree, so that the birds of the air come and perch in it"* (Matthew 13:31–32). Eventually, according to other scriptures (i.e. 2 Thessalonians 2:7–8), there will be a "showdown" between the Source of evil and the King of God's kingdom, in which Satan will be overthrown and Christ will reign.

---

56   Keller, *Center Church*, 229.

In this brief introduction to the subject, it's evident that understanding the difference between the church and the "kingdom"
may be a helpful means of providing a greater sense of freedom in
the way followers of Jesus see their role in the world in these times.
Men and women can serve in God's kingdom work without giving
a great deal of attention, for example, to gender role distinctions.
But when it comes to the church, it appears that closer attention
needs to be given to its structure because of its formative leadership
role within the development of the kingdom. Perhaps that is why
some leadership roles and callings in the church, biblically speaking, appear to be more limited. Yet it is evident too that all believers
in Jesus are called to be full participants in Christ's church (in its
various geographical locations), and should serve in it based on
their spiritual gifts and available time. But at the same time, all followers of Jesus should also seek to understand how God wishes to
use them in the larger community by their presence, words, and
deeds, in the expansion of Christ's kingdom. Some will be called
to work in specific Christian humanitarian ministries of compassion and social justice. Many more will be called to represent Christ
in their fields of secular employment and work expertise. At the
same time, the local church itself, under its leadership, should seek
to do various community ministries of mercy while continuously
maintaining its primary commitment to gospel-centered service in
those contexts.

Wrapping Up

Almost two millennia have passed since Jesus ascended to heaven and sent his Spirit to establish the church. Through many epochs of world history, by variations of progress and regress, it appears the number of professed Christians has steadily grown to more than thirty per cent of the world's population, the largest religious faith by almost ten per cent. Though the actual number of true believers is only known to God himself, and despite all the difficulties, Christ's promise to successfully build his church is indisputable.

From the human perspective, the church is not some monolithic unified structure as was once imagined under the Roman Empire. With the emergence of the Reformation at the dawn of the modern era, a new kind of intellectual freedom opened the door to a renewed understanding of biblical authority and interpretation. Inevitably, this latter development also birthed a large variety of Christian churches and denominations. Though denominationalism has mitigated Christ's call to practical unity, one positive outcome is that the development has served to balance theological extremes. At the least, the denominationalist trend illustrates the significance and impact of the cultural and theological shifts that have continuously affected the church. One of the biggest ongoing challenges for Christians around the world has always been how to manage the effect of cultural change on theological thought and Christian practice.

This book has been a modest attempt, from a pastoral perspective, to try to explain something of the enormous philosophical and cultural shift that has taken place in the Western world in the last fifty years. It has also been of special interest to note how this change has impacted the church, especially as it exists in its evangelical form. It is evident to many that postmodernism is now a dominant philosophical system that can't help but explain the reason for a growing skepticism regarding the Christian faith as well as a burgeoning secularism. It helps clarify why there has been a general decline of spiritual response to the Christian message, especially among the generation of people that has emerged in this time.

It's also evident that this philosophical and cultural shift is not all bad news. All is far from lost in this change. Even in these beginning stages of postmodernism, there are indications that amid the obvious feeling of chaos and despair, there is also a growing sense of genuine spiritual hunger. As described in these pages, in many ways postmodernism offers some refreshing relief from the cold intellectualism and formalism of the modern period. We would do well to enthusiastically welcome the greater interest in emotion, in personal transparency, in compassion, and in the desire for true justice. It is heartwarming to see the advent of a generation that is deeply sensitive to how people relate to our natural environment and to those who suffer. We should be encouraged by the deeper interest that we often see among a new generation toward true Christian discipleship, as well as to the work of the Holy Spirit.

Conservative evangelical Christians especially need to be careful lest they "throw out the baby with the bathwater." There is much in this new philosophical trend that commends it to what we understand as an ardent Christian faith. Thankfully, even though there has been an increase in practical atheism, there are still large pockets of young people in the Western world who are taking the call of Christ to a whole new level. But the focus has changed a bit. The trend is away from the more institutional forms of Christianity towards the Christian faith as a spiritual movement. It is less about the institutional church and more about the kingdom of God. In the words of Frost and Hirsch, it is more about going out than expecting them to come in. It is more about truly serving the needs of the world instead of about serving ourselves. And there is much in this notion that is very positive.

However, in my opinion, there are also some definite weaknesses in the current trend that the church must take pains to avoid. By far, the most serious effect of postmodernism has been the apparent headlong abandonment of the whole concept of objective truth. No doubt this is largely due to the tendency to lose sight of the transcendent nature of God (i.e. his existence apart from the world), and humanity's sense of accountability towards him. Just as modernism's man-centered proficiency has failed to satisfy Western man's true spiritual quest, postmodernism also has failed because it refuses to make a distinction between human existence and objective reality. Culturally, we have come to believe that any conception of reality outside ourselves is nothing more than our own imaginations. In postmodernism, the idea that humans through language arbitrarily assign meaning to conceptions of divinity, also fits well with thoughts of self-determination through a long evolutionary process of the origins of life and human development.

A secondary concern is all about emerging attitudes about the nature of the church. The anti-institutional nature of postmodernism tends to overlook the importance of the church as a biblical entity that is foundational to God's much larger kingdom development. The local church is the place for defined participation and membership through baptism and communion. It is a place for the development of a specific community in Christ and the main tenants of the Christian faith. It is in the local church that individuals and whole families are regularly instructed about biblical theology and Christian discipleship. It is through the church that its participants are initially prepared for service in God's larger kingdom work. Through its spiritually ordained leadership, people of all ages are discipled, equipped, and commissioned to do God's work in the world. It is my conviction that without the local church, God's larger kingdom work would soon fall into disarray. Today's Christian postmoderns should be careful lest they substitute God's kingdom development for the existence of the local church. Keeping this in mind, I believe, the evangelical church today needs to be diligent about helping to identify future pastors for the work of church leadership as well as providing the professional educational means by which they are able to prepare well for this kind of service.

With the abandonment of the notion of truth as objective reality, the most obvious alternative has been for people to rely upon their own instincts about the nature of life, its meaning, and how people should live in relation to one another. In the end, this is proving to be somewhat disheartening and contradictory. Just yesterday, I read about an interviewer who was asking university students about how they felt about someone of the opposite sex using the other's bathrooms in a public setting.[57] Everyone interviewed agreed that

---

57 Backholm, Joseph, College Kids Say the Darndest Things: On Identity, Youtube, 4:13. April 13, 2016, https://www.youtube.com/watch?v=xfOlveFs6Ho.

this kind of behaviour should not be censored. People should be given the right to make up their own minds about how they want to identify. But then the interviewer went on to ask the same individuals what they would think if the interviewer said he was of Chinese descent (which he obviously wasn't), or if he wanted to register as a student in a first-grade public school class, or if he said he was six feet, five inches tall (which again he obviously was not). Though the interviewees found the questions strange, they were reticent to say that the interviewer's questions were ridiculous! This illustrates how today's young adult generation, under the influence of cultural postmodernism, is unwilling to make any kind of commitment to that which is objectively true, because it might imply personal judgement of one kind or another.

The reality of this mind-set has profound implications for the future of Western society in general, and for the ministry of the church in particular. These are challenging days in which to seek to represent biblical truth. This very day, my regular Bible reading led me to a passage from 2 Timothy 4:1–4, in which Saint Paul writes some of his final words to Timothy and to the church.

> I charge you in the presence of God and of Christ
> Jesus, who is to judge the living and the dead,
> and by his appearing and his kingdom: preach
> the word, be ready in season and out of season;
> reprove, rebuke, and exhort, with complete
> patience and teaching. For the time is coming
> when people will not endure sound teaching,
> but having itching ears they will accumulate for
> themselves teachers to suit their own passions,
> and will turn from listening to the truth and
> wander off into myths.

It seems in greater ways than ever that we are beginning to experience what Saint Paul described in this brief exhortation to the young pastor, Timothy. If Paul's warning was relevant to Timothy so many centuries ago, his words seem even more applicable to pastors working with today's postmodern generation. While seeking to be relevant in legitimate ways, pastors need to be careful to guard against the tendency to accommodate themselves to the nuances of a cultural philosophy and practice that is basically opposed to truth claims.

One sure way to remain committed to truth as objective reality while at the same time retaining an incredible sense of relevance to culture is to understand the centrality and significance of the original gospel of Jesus Christ. Jesus' importance as a towering figure on the landscape of human history is undisputed even by secular historians. And the New Testament has proven to be a reliable historical document that lends a great deal of credence to details about his amazing life, unusual death, and astounding resurrection. The Christian metanarrative that provides the context for Jesus' life and work is a reasonable account, the strength of which is grounded in a remarkably unified record, even though it was written by many different authors over a period of fourteen hundred years. The climax of that record is the establishment of the church through the arrival of Jesus Christ and his announcement of the advent of the kingdom of God through his death and resurrection for the forgiveness of sin. Against all naysayers, throughout history and in these postmodern times, nothing ultimately makes more sense. And it's evident that many postmoderns also have embraced this message.

In each church in which I have served as a transition pastor, I have encountered many young people and newly-married couples who demonstrate that they have a deep personal commitment and relationship with the triune God and are passionate about the truth of the good news of Jesus. I'm thinking, for example, of a couple of individuals who served as pastoral ministry interns with me while I worked with the Erindale Alliance Church in Saskatoon. They proved to be uncompromising in their commitment to the gospel and became deeply engaged in helping junior and high school young people, as well as young adults in that church understand the gospel, helping them to grow in their relationship with Jesus and to live out the implications of the gospel.

I have seen that same spirit of love for God and commitment to the truth of the gospel among a group of young adults in the Cranbrook Alliance Church with which I also worked. They were deeply committed to reaching their peers and high school young people with the gospel. Several gave up their temporary jobs and other educational opportunities, that might have led to good financial security, in order to pursue by faith, a deeper understanding of what it meant to be a true disciple of Jesus Christ. In retrospect, it's evident that God has blessed these forays of faith and richly rewarded them, providing not only wonderful adventures in the Christian faith, but also meaningful personal relationships, as well as a better sense of what they are called to do in life.

Right now, I am serving in a small rural community in central British Columbia, where this same spirit of gospel commitment is evident among high school teen-age youth, young adults, and newly established families. In one case, after some years of following his own selfish interests (despite his participation in the church from birth), a young married man discovered the wonder of the gospel and what it meant to have a personal relationship with Jesus Christ. A few years ago, he gave up his good paying forestry job to pursue a full-time Bible education by correspondence. Having successfully completed that program, he is now preparing to move his wife and young family to a well-known seminary in the United

States for deeper biblical and theological studies in order to eventually serve as a full-time pastor. During his recent studies in this community, he and a few others have led a regular Bible study for young men, some of whom are new believers and followers of Jesus.

So, if through this book, you have had the impression that Christianity is close to being all but dead, nothing could be further from the truth. While the challenges to Christian faith and service are greater in our western culture due to postmodernism, and while it's true that there has been a significant degree of decline in church participation, Jesus Christ, just as he promised, continues to build his church through the presence and power of the Spirit. In my view, the western world could well be positioned for a great biblical Christian revival. If so, it will undoubtedly take place through millennials who have grown weary of the despair that postmodernism implies and are moved to recapture the true meaning of the gospel for our times.

The reader can catch the meaning of what I'm writing about by listening to some of the worship music of today's generation. This has been my experience in recent months as I have listened, for example, on YouTube, to the words of songs like, "This Is Amazing Grace."[58] There are many songs, like this one, that combine passion and unapologetic commitment to the meaning and proclamation of the gospel.

It's been suggested that postmodernism has already begun to experience its own demise. If that is so, no doubt it is because it

---

58 Wickham, Phil, Josh Farro, Jeremy Riddle, This Is Amazing Grace, *YouTube*, 4:39. November 13, 2013, https://www.youtube.com/watch?v=XFRjr_x-yxU.

offers no explanation to the deep desire that people universally
hold for a meaningful metanarrative. Despite all the naysayers,
Christianity through the gospel continues to offer the most satisfying explanation that the world has ever heard. And that is why the
church is continuing to grow at such a rapid rate in other parts of
the world. The reason the church faces opposition on every hand
is not because the gospel doesn't make good sense, but because it
systematically confronts humanity's predilection to live at odds
with the Creator. As John writes in his gospel, "*This is the verdict:
Light has come into the world, but people loved darkness instead of
light because their deeds were evil. Everyone who does evil hates the
light, and will not come into the light for fear that their deeds will be
exposed*" (John 3:19, 20 NIV). Conflict with, and opposition to
Christianity in its various forms will continue to exist because of
this reality. Therefore, the problem is not postmodernism, which
potentially merely represents one form of opposition, but the universal human condition.

Hopefully, this account of the change from modernism to postmodernism has given the reader new insight into the current reality
in western culture. If so, it is my hope and prayer that readers will
also have a growing desire to study this change further, and to
determine by God's grace how it's possible to make a difference
through the power of the gospel.

Bibliography

Appelo, Jurgen. *Virginia Satir Change Curve*. Licensed by Creative Commons. Google Image, accessed on January 2, 2017. https://www.flickr.com/photos/jurgenappelo/5201852636.

Backholm Joseph. *College Kids Say the Darndest Things: On Identity*, Youtube, 4:13. April 13, 2016, https://www.youtube.com/watch?v=xfO1veFs6Ho.

Backholm Joseph. *College Kids Say the Darndest Things: On Identity*, Youtube, 4:13. April 13, 2016, https://www.youtube.com/watch?v=xfO1veFs6Ho.

Biehl, Bob. *Masterplanning*. Mount Dora, FL: Aylen Publishing, 2005.

Bridges, William. *Transitions: Making Sense of Life's Changes*. Cambridge, MA: De Capo Press, 2004.

Bright, Bill. *The Four Spiritual Laws*. San Bernardino, CA: Campus Crusade for Christ, 1956.

Brown, Chris. *Religion in Canada: Are We Godless*. National News. Directed by Peter Mansbridge. May 13, 2015. Toronto: Canadian Broadcast Corporation, 2015. Television.

Canada. Parliament. House of Commons. "Marriage." Edited Hansard Debates. 36th Parl., 1st Session. Number 240. (June 8, 1999), http://www.ourcommons.ca/DocumentViewer/en/36-1/house/sitting-240/hansard.

Carson, D. A. *The Gagging of God: Christianity Confronts Pluralism.* Grand Rapids, MI: Zondervan, 1996.

Carson, D. A. *Becoming Conversant with the Emerging Church.* Grand Rapids, MI: Zondervan, 2005.

"Charitable Giving Statistics." *National Philanthropic Trust.* Accessed January 3, 2017. https://www.nptrust.org/philanthropic-resources/charitable-giving-statistics/.

"Civil Marriage Act." *Justice Laws Website, Government of Canada.* Accessed January 2, 2017. https://lop.parl.ca/About/Parliament/LegislativeSummaries/bills_ls.asp?ls=c38&Parl=38&Ses=1.

"Constitution Act 1982, Part I, Canadian Charter of Rights and Freedoms." *Justice Laws Website, Government of Canada.* Accessed January 2, 2017. http://laws-lois.justice.gc.ca/eng/Const/page-15.html.

Darling, Daniel. "Most College Students are Leaving the Church; Here's How This Church is Bucking the Trend." *Christianity Today: The Local Church,* October 20, 2016. Accessed on January 4, 2017. https://churchhealthwiki.wordpress.com/2016/10/21/oikos-evangelism-most-college-students-are-leaving-the-church-heres-how-this-congregation-is-bucking-the-trend/.

Demarest, Bruce. *Satisfy Your Soul.* Colorado Springs, CO: NavPress, 1999.

DeYoung, Kevin, and Ted Kluck. *Why We're Not Emergent.* Chicago: Moody Publishers, 2008.

Dirks, Morris. *Forming the Leader's Soul: An Invitation to Spiritual Direction.* Portland, OR: SoulFormation, 2013.

Drewlo, Edwin F. "Pastoral Care that Minimizes Negative Transition for Pastors of the C&MA Canada." Doctor of Ministry Dissertation. Trinity International University, 2005.

Drewlo, Edwin F. "Second Wind Ministries." http://www.secondwindministries.ca.

Engel, James F. "Engel's Scale." Google image. Accessed January 6, 2017. https://nukelearfishing.files.wordpress.com/2013/08/engel-scale.jpg.

Foster, Richard. *Celebration of Discipline.* San Francisco: Harper Collins, 1978.

Frost, Michael and Alan Hirsch. *The Shaping of Things to Come.* Peabody, MA: Hendrickson Publishers, 2003.

"Grounds of Discrimination." *Human Rights Complaints.* Government of Canada. Accessed January 2, 2017. http://www.canada.pch.gc.ca/eng/1448633333941/1448633333943#a2a.

Guinness, Os. *Fools Talk: The Art of Christian Persuasion.* Downers Grove, Ill: InterVarsity Press, 2015.

Gumble, Nicky. Home page. *Holy Trinity Brompton.* Accessed January 3, 2016. https://www.htb.org/.

Harrison William. *In Praise of Mixed Religion; The Syncretism Solution in a Multifaith World.* Montreal: McGill-Queen's University Press, 2014.

Keller, Timothy. *Center Church: Doing Balanced, Gospel-Centered Ministry in Your City*. Grand Rapids: Zondervan, 2012.

Keller, Timothy. *Making Sense of God: An Invitation to the Skeptical*. New York: Viking/Penguin Random House LLC, 2016.

McGavran, Donald, and Peter Wagner. *Understanding Church Growth*. Grand Rapids, MI: Erdmann's Publishing, 1970.

McKnight, Scot. *The King Jesus Gospel: The Original Good News Revisited*. Grand Rapids: Zondervan Pub, 2011.

McLaren, Brian. *A Generous Orthodoxy*. El Cajon, CA: Youth Specialties, 2004.

McQuilkin, Robertson, and Bradford Mullen. "The Impact of Post-Modern Thinking on Evangelical Hermeneutics." *Journal of the Evangelical Theological Society*, 40 no. 1. March 1997.

Newbigin, Lesslie. *Foolishness to the Greeks: the Gospel and Western Culture*. Grand Rapids, MI: Eerdmans, 1986.

Nouwen, Henri. *Reaching Out*. New York: Bantam Doubleday Dell, 1975.

Pew Research Center. "Canada's Changing Religious Landscape." *pewforum.org*. June 27, 2013. http://www.pewforum.org/2013/06/27/canadas-changing-religious-landscape/.

Pew Research Center. "America's Changing Landscape." *pewforum.org*. May 12, 2015. http://www.pewforum.org/2015/05/12/americas-changing-religious-landscape/.

Piper, John. *When I Don't Desire God: How to Fight for Joy*. Wheaton, Ill: Crossway Books, 2004.

Putnam, Robert D, and David E. Campbell, *American Grace: How Religion Divides and Unites Us*. New York: Simon and Schuster, 2010. Quoted in Tim Keller. *Center Church: Doing*

Balanced, Gospel-Centered Ministry in Your City. Grand Rapids: Zondervan, 2012.

Scazzero, Peter. *The Emotionally Healthy Church.* Grand Rapids, MI: Zondervan, 2003.

Shaeffer, Francis. *Escape from Reason.* London: Inter-varsity Press, 1968.

Simpson, A. B. *The Lord for the Body.* Harrisburg, PA: Christian Publications, 1959.

Shigematsu, Ken. *God in My Everything: How an Ancient Rhythm Helps Busy People Enjoy God.* Grand Rapids MI: Zondervan, 2013.

Thompson, Marjorie. *Soul Feast.* Louisville, KY: John Knox Press, 1995.

Veith, Gene. *Postmodern Times: A Contemporary Guide to Thought and Culture.* Wheaton, Ill: Crossway Books, 1994.

Wickham, Phil, Josh Farro, Jeremy Riddle. *This Is Amazing Grace, YouTube,* 4:39. November 13, 2013, https://www.youtube.com/watch?v=XFRjr_x-yxU.

Willard, Dallas. *Renovation of the Heart.* Colorado Springs, CO: NavPress, 2002.

"Wine Consumption in the U.S." *Wine Institute.* Accessed on January 3, 2017. https://www.wineinstitute.org/resources/statistics/article86.

Wright, Lisa. "Canada Among the Top Producers of Imported Wine." *Business, The Toronto Star.* February 17, 2015. https://www.thestar.com/business/2015/02/17/canada-among-the-worlds-top-consumers-of-imported-wine.html.

Wright, N. T. *Surprised by Hope: Rethinking Heaven, the Resurrection, and the Mission of the Church.* New York: Harper Collins, 2008.

Printed in Canada